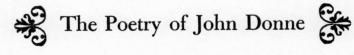

# The Poetry of John Donne

# THE
# POETRY
## OF
# JOHN DONNE
### *A Study in Explication*

BY

Doniphan Louthan

**BOOKMAN ASSOCIATES**
New York

*Printed in the U.S.A.*

NOBLE OFFSET PRINTERS, INC.
NEW YORK 3, N.Y.

... Thou [Earth] must audit on thy trust
Each graine and atome of this dust,
As thou wilt answer Him that lent,
Not gave thee my dear Monument.

—HENRY KING, *"The Exequy."*

# Foreword

THE PURPOSE OF this study is to examine the body of Donne's poems, to analyze a number of shorter poems and passages in detail, and to arrive at an evaluation of Donne's work in general. An attempt is made to distinguish Donne the poet from Donne the priest and Donne the person—however interesting the latter may be in their own right. The principal thesis of this study is a somewhat negative one: that many misconceptions of Donne criticism are due directly to superficial reading of the poems, and importation of patterns which patently do not fit them. This essay makes no pretense of being a highpowered product of the New Criticism.

In its original form, this study was a dissertation presented for the degree of Doctor of Philosophy in Yale University. The dissertation was written under the direction of Mr. Cleanth Brooks, to whose writings and personal guidance I am highly indebted. I should mention the fact, however, that I am not a duly accredited disciple of Mr. Brooks. He should not be saddled with opinions which are mine but not his.

At Yale I was also indebted to Mr. Helge Kökeritz, with his immense store of knowledge on phonological matters; and to Mr. René Wellek, who oriented me on theory of literature.

I should also like to record a debt to Mr. Austin Warren, of the University of Michigan. This project was inspired in part by Mr. Warren's stimulating classroom lectures on Donne, at Kenyon School of English, the summer of 1948.

And I am extremely grateful for the patience and industry of my wife, Anne Dannemiller Louthan, who helped me at every stage of composition and preparation for the press. I, of course, am solely responsible for the shortcomings of the essay.

I am gateful to the following publishers for permission to

reprint material from the books listed below. HARCOURT, BRACE AND COMPANY: *Selected Esayss* 1917-1932, by T. S. Eliot; *The Well Wrought Urn: Studies in the Structure of Poetry,* by Cleanth Brooks; *Theory of Literature,* by René Wellek and Austin Warren. NEW DIRECTIONS: *Seven Types of Ambiguity,* Second Edition, by William Empson. NEW DI- RECTIONS and CHATTO & WINDUS: *Some Versions of Pastoral,* by William Empson. OXFORD UNIVERSITY PRESS: *A Study of the Prose Works of John Donne,* by Evelyn M. Simpson. RANDOM HOUSE and NONESUCH PRESS: *John Donne. . . . : Complete Poetry and Selected Prose,* edited by John Hayward. STANFORD UNIVERSITY PRESS: *A Sermon Preached at Lincoln's Inn by John Donne,* edited by George R. Potter. UNIVERSITY OF NORTH CAROLINA PRESS: *Modern Poetry and the Tradition,* by Cleanth Brooks.

D. L.

# Contents

# 1

# An Invocation to the Donne Canon

CHARLES LAMB ONCE referred to the meaning of Donne's poems as *"uncomeatable* . . . without a personal citation from the dead."[1]* The situation is perhaps not so desperate as all that. We cannot assemble each atom of Donne's mortal dust, to interview him on the meaning of his poems, but—until such is possible—we can (and sometimes must) audit each atom of evidence which has come down to us, in the effort to clarify his meaning, before going on (if need be) to determine values to which his conscious meaning is irrelevant. Specifically, we must often study each atom in the structure of a poem, and each poem in the context of the canon. Sometimes we will need a prose citation from Donne the priest or Donne the person, but we will almost certainly have to disentangle Donne's poetry from his public or private life.

As a research project, this essay received the title "Studies in

* This is the first and only footnote in this essay. Superior numbers refer to notes appearing in the section which begins on p.176, below. These notes are purely bibliographical (sources of quotations, places and dates of publication, etc.). I have due respect for documentation, but rebel against the idea of a reader's tripping over a footnote every ten words. One parenthetical passage, however, has proved too long for inclusion in the body of the essay, and hence appears as the Appendix.

the Text and the Meaning of Donne's Shorter Poems." The
reference to text might be misleading; no effort is made here
to establish a new apparatus criticus. My assumption is merely
that the text is the meaning, and the meaning is the text—an
assumption in no way original. Even the most casual student of
Donne knows that almost every word may be integral in his
poems; slight tampering with the text may change the meaning
radically. As everyone knows, practically all of Donne's poems
were published posthumously, and we have no autograph MSS.
of the poems. There *are* extant, however, a number of 17 c.
MSS. and printed editions—and, consequently, a number of
variant readings. While external evidence permits us to separate
improbabilities from probabilities, we must ultimately resort to
literary (i.e., esthetic) criteria in choosing between one variant
reading and another. There are enough undisputed passages for
us to arrive at what is and what is not characteristically Donne-
ian. (I am quite willing to grant that some readings may represent early stages of composition; I am interested, however, in
presenting only what I consider the nearest approximation to
Donne's final text.)

Sir Herbert Grierson's monumental edition of 1912 is still
basic for the study of Donne's poems. His apparatus criticus has
held up remarkably well, and it would be inaccurate to say that
his explanatory notes are outmoded. No one before Grierson
took such pains to explicate the poems, and every succeeding
critic is apt to be highly indebted to him, as I undoubtedly am,
but there are still gaps in Grierson's explication. Sometimes
Grierson is wrong; sometimes he is misleading; often, however,
he arrives at his text and his notes by means of analysis, but fails
to present the analysis for our inspection. We have to go through
the process ourselves to find out whether his choice is valid.
At any rate, he considers many things obvious which we would
like to see explained.

# An Invocation to the Donne Canon

The significance of the title to this chapter should presently be evident. I am *not*—let it be said here—concerned with establishing the canon of Donne's poetry. Explication is the problem involved. This essay will cover individually only a select number of the shorter poems, will attempt to make their meaning clear, and will try to set up cautionary principles against misreading Donne. (It must also arrive at some sort of general evaluation.) In the interests of minimizing boredom in the reader, few analyses will attempt word-by-word explication. The selection of poems may or may not be considered representative. They have this in common, at least: most of the poems are fairly difficult to interpret, and most of them are worth the effort. (In auditing each atom, this essay admittedly runs the danger of being atomistic.)

There are a good many things to be said in favor of the subjective approach to poetry. James Thurber, I suppose, has put the case most wittily.[2] Thurber cites with delighted approval certain gross (though not vulgar) misreadings of Byron, and—along similar lines—a youngster's misconception of the Lord's Prayer: "Our Father, who art in Heaven, Halloween be Thy name." The trouble with subjectivity is that it tends to bore other people. Unfortunately or otherwise, literary scholarship is hardly an exact science, but there are ways of minimizing subjectivity. In the specific case of Donne, scholarship and criticism can provide the following safeguards against subjective interpretation:

1. Evidence of accepted grammatical patterns and structure in the time of Donne.
2. Evidence of dictionary meanings in the period, with NED references supplemented to the extent possible.
3. Testimony of the textual critic.
4. Background of philosophical concepts in Donne's time.
5. Consensus of Donne's verse and prose, as to attitudes and

meanings expressed in words and metaphors which appear in multiple contexts.

6. Architectonics of Donne's metaphors, and of his poetic structure in general, by which atypical readings would be suspect. The drift or direction of the whole poem, is of importance in this connection.

No matter how conscientiously I utilize these safeguards, of course, I confidently expect accusations of subjectivity. It is the sort of charge I will probably make many times in this essay, against both scholars and critics (though mainly against critics, who stick their necks out farther). I have no pretext for taking affront, when I am accused myself.

In the analyses here, no attempt will be made to cite all previous commentators on particular poems. The choice of critics to agree or disagree with, is admittedly an act of critical judgment. Some critics are hardly worth refuting, and many scholarly articles are so peripheral as to be worthless in any analysis of esthetic qualities. It is quite possible, however, that I have neglected significant commentaries. I foresee disagreement with three classes of Donne enthusiasts:

1. Writers of fictional biography. This class is not confined to biographers proper: critics, scholars, and biographers, alike, have a tendency to indulge in subjective reconstructions based on a superficial reading of the poems. Hugh I'A. Fausset is perhaps the worst offender in this group.[3]
2. Poetic theorists who find what they want to find in Donne. I am not prepared to cite a worst offender, but the fault is that of over-reading. In the Appendix (for example), I point out what I consider an over-reading on the part of William Empson.
3. Cultural historians who claim Donne for Medievalism or Renaissance Modernism or Platonism or Naturalism. The cultural history is generally sound, but the writers are characteristically weak in showing how Donne fits into the

pattern. The worst offenders err through superficial reading of the poems.

My own weakness inclines me towards the second class, though I would like to be erudite enough to qualify for the third.

This section might well close with what seems to be Donne's own comment on subjective interpretation. The ninth stanza of *The Litanie* is our text:

### THE APOSTLES

And thy illustrious Zodiacke
Of twelve Apostles, which ingirt this All,
    From whom whosoever do not take
Their light, to darke deep pits, throw downe, and fall,
        As through their prayers, thou'hast let mee
                    know
        That their bookes are divine;
May they pray still, and be heard, that I goe
Th'old broad way in applying; O decline
Mee, when my comment would make thy word mine.

(Ll. 73-81.)

Here the deity is entreated to throw down and fall (i.e., fell) those mortals who are not prudent enough to take the apostles' light "to darke deep pits." These errant ones are not necessarily to be thrown into the pits, but they are to be humiliated and shown their imprudence. The poet asks the same treatment for himself, in the event that he departs from the teachings of the apostles' books (which are divine books). The "old broad way" is the main highway—God's intended path for men. *Decline* means *to deflect* (from the wrong path: the subjective interpretation of God's word), but also *to humiliate* (call back to one's senses) and—above all—*to inflect grammatically* (substitute the second person for the first). The personal pronoun is to undergo change from *me* to *thou;* the pronominal adjetcive, from *my* (*word*) to *thy* (*word*).

In Donne's spirit we might invoke the aid of his canon (the songs and sonnets canonized by love); we could wish the canon to decline *us,* when our commentary would make *its* word *ours.*

## 2

Several pages to follow will be devoted to a topic which might read: "Approaches to the Study of Imagery in the Metaphysical Lyrics of Donne." I have deliberately chosen this wording because it concentrates a number of red herrings into a single phrase.

*Imagery* is the first red herring I would mention. An image, by definition (or at least by semantic implication), is visualizable to the mind's eye. But Donne's figures seldom lend themselves readily to visualization. To be sure, Donne's famous compass figure may have had its origin in the design which served as the imprint of the Plantin Press,[4] but Donne's figure is considerably more complex and difficult to visualize than this simple emblem of constancy. John Crowe Ransom has commented on the inadequacy of point-to-point correspondences in the compass figure.[5] My own version is slightly different; here I will merely cite the extended analysis of "A Valediction: forbidding mourning," which appears in Chapter 2, below.

From a mechanical, statistical point of view (on the basis of image-sources), one may study Donne's imagery in much the same manner as Shakespeare's. Indeed, Milton A. Rugoff and Miss Caroline Spurgeon take somewhat similar approaches to Donne and Shakespeare, respectively (comments in Rugoff's book will be discussed in detail later).[6] But the study of Donne's imagery ultimately involves a distinction of his type of poetry from other types with other modes of imagery.

I consequently pass to the second red herring: *Metaphysical.*

# An Invocation to the Donne Canon

I am not here concerned with the adequacy or inadequacy of such labels as "Metaphysical" and "baroque," or with all the tortuous efforts which have been made to differentiate Donne's type of poetry from other types. In the reviews of Miss Rosemond Tuve's book on *Elizabethan and Metaphysical Imagery*,[7] one repeatedly encounters the complaint that Miss Tuve has failed to distinguish adequately between Spenser's (or Sidney's) and Donne's type of poetry. To overstate cruelly, Miss Tuve virtually declares that Donne is like Spenser, only more so. I am inclined to agree with René Wellek that "The most convincing analysis [of Metaphysical or baroque technique] is a variation and elaboration of Dr. Johnson's suggestion that '*discordia concors*: a combination of dissimilar images, or discovery of occult resemblances in things apparently unlike' is characteristic of metaphysical wit."[8]

*Lyrics* is the last red herring. I want to consider two ways in which it is confusing as applied to Donne. In the first place, we think of lyrics as being singable. Now, poems like "Goe, and catch a falling starre . . . " and "Sweetest love, I do not goe . . ." are " pure" or "poetic" poems in the best Elizabethan-lyric tradition. There is extant music to go with some of Donne's poems, but we feel that most of the poems are more colloquial than "lyrical." Complex imagery tends to make for complex rhythmical patterns. When we hear certain of the Holy Sonnets performed as set to music by Benjamin Britten, we are reminded very strongly of operatic recitative. Donne's characteristic poetry is far from being *lyrical* in the sense of *eminently singable*.

But it is the second confusion arising from the word *lyric* to which I wish to devote most attention, with reference to imagery. Lyrical poetry is often thought of as *personal, "sincere"* poetry. The extent to which Donne's poems are personal history is still a very vexed question. I am immediately concerned here with the interrelationships between the question of Donne's

19

imagery and the matter of sincerity—ultimately connected with the problem of belief.

Mr. Austin Warren comments on one way in which imagery and sincerity may be subjects of the same investigation:

> The assumption that a poet's imagery is the central contribution of his unconscious and that in it, therefore, the poet speaks as a man, not as an artist, seems, in turn, referable back to floating, not very consistent, assumptions about how to recognize "sincerity." On the one hand, it is popularly supposed that striking imagery must be contrived, and hence insincere: a man really moved would either speak in a simple unfigured language or in banal and faded language. But there is a rival idea that the trite figure evoking the stock response is a sign of insincerity, of accepting a crude approximation to one's feeling in place of a scrupulous statement of it. Here we confuse men generally with literary men, men talking with men writing, or, rather, men talking with poems. Ordinary personal candor and trite imagery are eminently compatible. As for "sincerity" in a poem: the term seems almost meaningless. A sincere expression of what? Of the supposed emotional state out of which it came? Or of the state in which the poem was written? Or a sincere expression of the poem, i. e., the linguistic construct shaping in the author's mind as he writes? Surely it will have to be the last: the poem is a sincere expression of the poem.[9]

Any study of imagery is questionable which is primarily interested in sneaking up on the blind side of the poet as person.

This is not the place to multiply examples of the biographical or personal heresy—that crudest of analogues to the sinceritas heresy. Many a Donne scholar has found it desirable to follow the saint's-life pattern which Walton set up. Thus we would peg down poems according to events in Donne's life; the sequence would run from the hedonistic indiscretions of the young Jack Donne to the elevated spirituality of Dr. Donne the divine (Walton had virtually ignored Jack Donne's existence).

This method neatly solves the problem of sincerity—or so it would seem—because the sensuality of the secular-love poems can be more than counterbalanced by the devotion of the Divine Poems, which presumably constitute a palinode.

Several difficulties crop up immediately. Evidence is worse than flimsy—in most cases—for the pinning down of poems to actual biographical events. Moreover, hovering in the background, there had been the idea of "striking imagery . . . as contrived, and hence insincere. . . ." Concede that Donne was sincerely sensual in his unreconstructed youth, and you still haven't solved the problem posed by sensuality. Assuming that the Divine Poems are personal, one cannot gainsay the cross-references to secular love, even as a thing of the past. Punning and downright-erotic imagery may be found in the Divine Poems. (Puns, incidentally, even appear in the Sermons.) A detailed discussion of the erotic imagery in certain Holy Sonnets, appears in Chapter 5, below. Notable puns occur in "A Hymne to God the Father" and "Hymne to God my God, in my sicknesse." In the former the poet puns on the name of the divinity (Son-Sun) and on his own name. In the latter, presumably composed on his very deathbed, there are parallel puns in Latin and English, on the concept of straitness—in addition to an ambiguity based on the word *purple*. The secular-love poems also cause considerable difficulty, since here the linking of secular with sacred love is amost explicit, and here the erotic imagery is most uninhibited.

Not even a tentative solution will be offered at this juncture, to the specific difficulties growing out of the problem of sincerity. Here it should be sufficient to quote T. S. Eliot on the subject:

. . . With sincerity in the practical sense, poetry has little to do; the poet is responsible to a much more difficult consciousness and honesty. And it is because he has this honesty, because he is so often expressing his genuine whole of tangled feelings, that Donne is, like the early Italians, like Heine, like Baudelaire, a poet of the world's literature.[10]

The problem of sincerity is one to which we shall return.

3

One of the basic principles of textual criticism is that of *difficilior lectio*. When a text has been tampered with in transmission, the more difficult of variant readings are usually to be preferred, since copyists have a tendency to "clarify" and over-simplify what they don't understand. In Donne's case the principle is especially useful, because his verse is unusually subtle. But the conscientious critic might well bear in mind—when dealing with Donne—the principle of *facilior lectio*. He should, in other words, choose the easiest reading the context will bear (whether or not there is a textual problem involved).

Hazlitt once remarked that Donne's thoughts were "delivered by the Caesarean operation."[11] Render unto Caesarean the things that are Caesarean's. We sometimes tend to feel that anything goes, in Donne—the most involved chain of thought, the most fantastic metaphor, the most outrageous ambiguity. We are on safe ground so long as we recognize this attitude as hyperbolical; when we take ourselves literally, we get into trouble. I would like to indicate, here, some things which *aren't* likely to happen in Donne—cases where the principle of *facilior lectio* is only prudent.

It is fairly obvious that, in the time of Shakespeare and Donne, certain words had underworld connotations. One of these was the verb *die,* which could mean *to attain a sexual orgasm.*[12] The semantic implications apparently have something to do with the primitive belief that vital spirits of the blood are wasted away by excessive breathing or excessive bodily discharges (like the sighing and weeping in Donne's "Sweetest love . . . ").[13] At any rate, sexual intercourse was supposed to cut down one's life expectancy in a radical manner (see Donne's "Farewell to love"); sexual consummation would be a sort of gradual dying. (There may be a semantic cross-reference to the insect world, of course; there, in certain species, fulfillment of reproductive function is followed immediately by death.)

This point once established, we should proceed with great caution. The fact that a sexual connotation is available, does not mean that one is present in every use of the verb *die*. Allen Tate, regarding a certain Donne passage, makes the mistake of assuming this semantic implication too readily, and the incidental mistake of postulating "a concealed pun" of a type I believe uncharacteristic of Donne. Tate quotes the first two stanzas of the Mourning valediction:

> As virtuous men passe mildly away,
>     And whisper to their soules, to goe,
> Whilst some of their sad friends doe say,
>     The breath goes now, and some say, no:
>
> So let us melt, and make no noise,
>     No teare-floods, nor sigh-tempests move,
> T'were prophanation of our joyes
>     To tell the layetie our love.
>                         (Ll. 1-8.)

According to Tate, "The elaborate simile here asserts on several planes the analogy between the act of love and the moment of death. . . . The analogy contains a concealed pun [on the erotic meaning of *die*].[14] Tate does not tell us how he knew that the sexual act was involved; we would need the "concealed pun" to tell us. I have grave doubts, however, about the likelihood of a pun on a word which never appears. Donne may pun on concepts (like that of dying), but he always or nearly always seems to do so through the medium of specific words (like *die* or the phonetic equivalent). Tate's reading is altogether out of tone.

There are other locations in Donne which frequently have erotic connotations. One is *secret parts,* but even that cannot be trusted to contain a sexual sub-meaning. In Donne's epistle "To Mr. S. B.," the term appears to be perfectly neutral, in the geographical sense *hidden regions.* —The phonological analysis of Donne's verse, neglected as the technique has been, offers many temptations to erotic and other misreadings. There is no substitute for close reading—for the auditing of each atom—in the attempt to distinguish between valid and invalid readings. Though I cannot present detailed structural analyses and phonological documentation here, I think it fairly obvious that "Loves Usury" and "Loves Alchymie" contain phonetic puns involving the word *whore.* "For every houre that thou wilt spare mee now," the former poem begins. *Hour* and *whore* undoubtedly were homonyms in Donne's time (there was more than one current pronunciation of *whore*).[15] The speaker of "Loves Usury" is seeking, not only time (every hour he can be spared), but opportunity (every whore available); at an advanced age he will have little use for either hours or whores.

Again, in "Loves Alchymie" there is a reference to "that dayes rude hoarse minstralsey." The speaker of the poem is disparaging the concept of Platonic love (among other things); if an exponent of the possibility of such love were logical, he would have to identify rude whores' minstrelsy with the harmony of the spheres.

I would like to offer an example—of my own fabrication—of how to go wrong with all the modern aids. In the Window valediction the speaker is ruminating on his name as inscribed on a window of his beloved's chamber. He concludes that ". . . glasse, and lines must bee,/No meanes our firme substantiall love

24

to keepe. . . ." This statement apparently means that the inscribed glass is a symbol inadequate to celebrate "our firme substantiall love," or that the name alone is incapable of preserving the present state of mutual fidelity .But the enthusiastic explicator can wring a great deal more out of this passage—perhaps even seduction propaganda of the type M. Legouis fancies.[16] *Glass* might be considered an erotic symbol, like *glass of virginity* in Shakespeare.[17] *Lines* might be interpreted as hiding a pun on the homonym *loins*.[18] Maidenhead and loins are inadequate to contain, to restrain our love for one another. (There's a divinity that shapes our ends.) This love is to be preserved by intercourse and (perhaps) by procreation.—The previous rumination has been "idle talke," but the speaker excuses himself on the grounds of deathbed dotage. He has been lying with his mistress and thinking out loud; his thinking has been fuzzy, because he has been about to die, in the erotic sense of the verb:

4

Neere death inflicts this lethargie,
And this I murmure in my sleepe;
Impute this idle talke, to that I goe,
For dying men talke often so.
(Ll. 63-66.)

The shortcomings of the reading above should be sufficiently evident.

What specific attitudes should we adopt toward the major divisions of Donne's poetry? The satires, the epistles, the occasional poems on marriage and on death—these are relatively conventional; i. e., our attitudes are more or less conditioned by the genre. We know approximately what to expect from satire, and so on. Even the Divine Poems may be accepted as personal lyrics of devotion, none the less reverent because they recognize the existence of physical love, and effect syntheses in "striking imagery." But for the secular-love poems, at least, we find it necessary to adopt the postulate of "dramatic monologue" (or, perhaps, "dramatic soliloquy," in the case of poems like "Communitie").

In Donne we find Petrarchan poems upholding Platonic love, and beside these, poems attacking (or exulting in) the sensual frailties of woman. In some poems the logic is flawless; in others it is obviously sophistical—even to the extent of being seduction propogranda on the part of the speaker. To reconcile these diversities of attack, and to get around the vulnerable theory of these "lyrics" as personal, modern critics have accepted the poems as dramatic monologues. Each poem has its self-contained situation, the solution being in terms of the situation, not in terms of extrinsic value-systems. Thus the individual image and the structure of a poem, if not typically coterminous (as John Crowe Ransom has imprudently suggested[19]) are at least analogous in function: the working out of an equipoise within a closed system.

W. B. Yeats once observed that out of the quarrel with others we make rhetoric—out of the quarrel with ouselves we make poetry.[20] An adaptation of this definition might well be applicable to Donne. Out of the quarrel with himself (if so we may call his trying on of moods and personalities), Donne made poetry which is rhetoric and logic—a dialectic which is none the less poetry. In the terms of our earlier quotation from Eliot, the poet is responsible for *this* type of sincerity: the accurate reporting of his quarrel.—With such a provisional summary we must be content for the time.

I am not altogether satisfied with my account of the major divisions of Donne's poetry. The fact is that it is not so much *my* account, as a consensus of what seem to be the current attitudes. We might arbitrarily divide into three parts, Donne's personality as poet:

1. The dramatic poet
2. The public poet
3. The personal poet

There are no such tidy lines of demarkation, of course. Chronology is not so obliging. The Satyres, for example—early though they are—belong to Donne's phase as public poet. The difference between the dramatic and the personal poet, is a matter which occupies much of this essay. We might well consider here the ways in which the public poet differs from the dramatic and the personal poet, alike. In general terms, first: The dramatic poet is not necessarily interested in presenting attitudes he holds as a person, while such is the sole concern of the personal poet. But the public poet is a sort of self-appointed laureate. His motives are not altogether esthetic, at times; he can improve his standard of living with a well-timed epithalamium or funeral elegy. This situation may or may not make him a hack. It undoubtedly will, if the product is purely mechanical, but public requirements may still leave room for poetic purposes.

High motives alone will not save a poem, but we like to feel that Donne's eulogy of various ladies is prompted by the search for an expression of ideal womanhood—his declared motive in praising the late Elizabeth Drury, whom he had never met.[21] Certainly, there were practical advantages to praising a great lady. If the ladies compared notes (as they evidently did), they found a number of their peers described in the superlative terms which, at best, one woman and only one could deserve.

Satires belong by convention to a sort of public classification; the ideas expressed in the Satyres may or may not be Donne's private sentiments. The verse-epistles, by virtue of being written in verse instead of prose, may assume a sort of public character, whether or not they seem to angle for patron-age. *An Anatomie of the World* apparently combined in its motivation the desire for economic reward, the aforementioned seeking after ideal womanhood, and Donne's seizing of the op-portunity to comment on his own times. Unlikely as it seems, there is structural similarity between the *Anatomie* and the little poem "The Feaver." In each the beloved one dies (actually or in fantasy), and the world promptly goes to pot in her absence. We may gauge the difference in approach of the poems, by ex-amining the ways in which the world goes to pot in each. There is certainly a major difference, for example, between the world as vaporing away with the first lady's breath, and the world as being beset with doubts arising from "the new philosophy," upon the death of Elizabeth Drury. In the larger work Donne as public poet is evaluating the civilization of his own times, whether or not he personally believes each attitude expressed. The blasphemy charge Ben Jonson leveled against the *Ana-tomie*,[22] indicates—I think—that the world-decay image in this poem was not accepted as the purely conventional figure which it is in other contexts. "A Feaver" would hardly have been ac-cused of blasphemy.

5

The following pages will deal with types of muting which are required in the reading of Donne. Two of these types in-volve, respectively, two separate senses of the term *vehicle*: the technical, Ricardian sense;[23] and a more ordinary sense, by which a neutral vehicle is a passage (a vehicle for statement) which accomplishes its desired effect without reference to the poet's personal belief in the imaginative terms used.

To get down to cases involving the more ordinary sense of *neutral vehicle*, Rugoff commits a major error, I think, when he manipulates his material in *Donne's Imagery* to support a cliché of Donne scholarship. The frequency of figures from trade and commerce, is offered as proof of "Donne's rejection of the Petrarchian and Spenserian conventions."[24] True, a choice of one thing must imply a rejection of another (others), but *rejection* is too strong a term for disinclination to choose something. Actually, Donne seems to use Petrarchan style when it suits his convenience to do so. New twists to Petrarchan imagery, need not imply a revolt against that type of imagery. (Cf. the discussion of "that happy busk" in "Elegie XIX," Chapter 3 below.)

The fact seems to be that training in (or long acquaintance with) patristic methods of exegesis, inclined Donne towards dialectical style, with all material grist for his mill. Everyone knows, moreover, that Donne was a victim of "the worst voluptuousnes, which is an Hydroptique immoderate desire of humane learning. . . ."[25] His wide ranging intellectual curiosity was not concerned with books alone, and in one sense he is among the least literary of poets. Rugoff, as a matter of fact, points out the scarcity of his allusions to classical mythology.

Though one may, like Charles M. Coffin,[26] use all available documentation to establish Donne's personal stand on science (and on superstitious beliefs of the time, etc., if enough external evidence is available), such information is not relevant to the interpretation of his poems, where something he doesn't believe in as a person may secure a desired imaginative effect for him. Whatever the difficulties of writing poetry (or merely of existing) in Donne's time, there was a certain advantage to living in a transitional period between medievalism and Renaissance modernism, despite the malaise caused by the new philosophy. Donne had wide leeway in the choice of imaginatively charged material for imagery. A twentieth-century poet would find it difficult to utilize (say) the Ptolemaic system imaginatively. Despite Ben Jonson's comments on Donne's obscurity,[27] we should be cautious in assuming that Donne's poetry—however difficult—was esoteric through reference to ancient beliefs no living person could possibly hold. As Rugoff notes, Donne drew imagery from any side of a controversial question. It is important to remember that the controversies were hardly dead issues in Donne's time. There were numerous living people who actually believed in angelology, for example; Donne was not just digging something up out of an old book.

Now for the technical sense of *neutral vehicle*. Utilizing the Ricardian division of metaphor into tenor and vehicle, we may say that Donne's vehicles need not modify in any way the tone of the tenors. An obvious example occurs in *An Anatomie of the World*, with reference to Elizabeth Drury:

> . . . As some Serpents poyson hurteth not,
> Except it be from the live Serpent shot,
> So doth her vertue need her here, to fit
> That unto us; shee working more then it.
> (Ll. 409-412.)

This, of course, is not strictly a metaphor, but the effect is metaphorical. The statement is that Elizabeth Drury's virtue has not died with her, but that her personal presence is needed to put it into effect among mortals. That statement is the tenor; the vehicle is a bit of incidental intelligence (erroneous, from the scientific point of view). There is no carry-over whatever of our attitude toward serpents' poison. Donne is not attacking a hated enemy; he is praising a young woman of consummate virtue (whether or not she is identical with the late Elizabeth Drury). (Nor can we imagine that—had Donne known better—he would have worried about the scientific inaccuracy in the poem; this passage is an example of both types of neutral vehicle.) The tone of the vehicle is neutral (*vehicle* is used here in the technical sense), yet paradoxically it lends concreteness and color to the somewhat pallid statement of the tenor alone. (Neutrality need not negate incongruity—the basis of the Metaphysical conceit; there would have been incongruity of a sort even if the serpent figure had been applied to a hated person. Try substituting *meanness* for *virtue* in this passage.)

Donne may use the same vehicle with different tenors—and quite different results. In the Mourning valediction the speaker and his beloved are to submit quietly to enforced separation, as virtuous men accept death quietly, so that witnesses cannot tell precisely when the end comes. In the Valentine epithalamium the bride is to remove her clothes and get into bed so fast that the stages of undressing are indistinguishable, "As Soules from bodies steale, and are not spy'd" (l. 78). The implicit clothing metaphor—body as garment of soul—is particularly effective here, of course. In the valediction the emphasis is somewhat different: Let's abandon our bodies quietly and exist in the spirit.

These are imaginative uses of the common belief that the virtuous die quietly. Donne the divine takes pains to refute the implications of the converse: " . . . Make no *ill conclusions* upon any mans *loathness to die.* . . ."[28] The difference here is not merely that Donne has entered the Church in the interim: the trueness or falsity of the folk belief is immaterial in the poem, but human behavior is involved in the exhortation of the sermon.

There are border-line cases where the neutrality of the vehicle is somewhat in question. In the funeral "Elegie on the Lady Marckham," we find this passage:

> In her this sea of death hath made no breach,
>     But as the tide doth wash the slimie beach,
> And leaves embroder'd workes upon the sand,
>     So is her flesh refin'd by deaths cold hand.
>                 (Ll. 17-20.)

According to the thought-content of the passage and its context, we should expect *slimie* to be neutral, with no application to the statement of the tenor. Knowing Donne, however, with his growing fondness for descriptions of decay in the grave, we suspect a certain amount of carry-over to the tenor.—Notice, here, the rapid shift from one figure to another—but without mixing of metaphor. The vehicle is an analogy (the tide beautifying the beach); the tenor, a metaphor (beautification by a sculptor's hand, perhaps)—this metaphor being a restatement of another—and rejected—metaphor (a dike pounded by the sea).

In certain passages of savage denunciation, a vehicle in Donne may abandon neutrality. Such is the case in his last sermon, where Donne is speaking of the various deaths we undergo in life:

. . . *Our birth dies* in *infancy,* and our *infancy* dies in *youth,* and *youth* and the rest die in *age,* and *age* also dies, and *determines all.* Nor doe all these, youth out of infancy, or age out of youth arise so, as a *Phoenix* out of the *ashes* of another *Phoenix* formerly *dead,* but as a *waspe* or a *serpent* out of a *caryon,* or as a *Snake* out of *dung.* Our *youth* is worse than our infancy, and our *age worse* than our *youth. . . .*[29]

The bare statement is that there is a certain continuity between the stages punctuated by death, but it is not the sort figured by the phoenix-myth of triumphant continuity in change. The ashes don't rise again: they decay and engender vermin. Here the vehicle is obviously emotive—as the context reveals, if the passage alone is not sufficient evidence. A similar type of savage denunciation may help to account for the minutely close interrelationship between tenor and vehicle which I find in the best-known crux of "Satyre II" (this poem is a special case, however; see Chapter 4, below).

Rugoff would have us believe that Donne consciously dislikes the conventional and the hackneyed (beyond his natural antipathy, as a poet in his senses, to effects deadened by overuse). It is certainly true that Donne employs shock-technique at times, and his imagery is far more unhackneyed than otherwise, but we may attribute the effect to Donne's freshness of approach—somewhat different from deliberate revolt against the conventional. There are times when conventional imagery suits his purpose—even when the imagery is used in a conventional way. In at least two of his sermons, Donne uses St. Paul's paradox of the mortal as putting on immortality. In one of these references, Donne's use of the expression is purely traditional (mortality as yielding to immortality);[30] in the other, there is a subtle paradox based on common knowledge of the Pauline paradox: ". . . If wee had not sinned in *Adam, mortality had not put on immortality,* (as the *Apostle* speakes) nor, *corruption had not put on incorruption,* but we had had our *transmigration* from this to the other world, without any *mortality,* any *corruption* at all."[31] Here it is possible to interpret the paradox in the traditional sense (mortality could not have yielded to immortality, since there would have been no mortality to begin with), but the passage is deliberately made to appear a misreading of St. Paul (so far as the human race is concerned, Adam's sin resulted in perpetual [immortal] mortality).

We have mentioned several types of muting which the reader must bring to Donne. One is that required by a neutral Ricardian vehicle (it may be maintained, however, that *neutral* is a misnomer: the tone of the vehicle may be thought of as neutralized abruptly, with a subsequent effect of paradox). Muting is also required after each figure in a rapid series, lest the effect be that of a mixed metaphor; Shakespeare (as in the "sea of troubles" passage) uses this technique more frequently than Donne. (The whole problem of mixed metaphor, however, requires further exploration.) As for potential erotic ambiguities, we may never know what cue to muting was used with Renaissance audiences (those without a text before them, to

33

help them determine delicate shadings of tone). In polite company we moderns (I trust) never think of certain words as potentially obscene, though we grasp the implication immediately when we hear them from a low-comedy entertainer. But the Age of Elizabeth was not particularly squeamish; Shakespeare and the nobility in his audience probably enjoyed—and admitted enjoying—his bawdy jokes as much as the groundlings did. Ill-timed guffaws at the verb *die*, must have occurred rather frequently, though even the groundlings were probably much better prepared for poetic drama than their modern counterparts are. (This situation must have been complicated by the use of *die* with both wit and high seriousness, as in Juliet's speech at the tomb.[32]) This historical probability is no excuse for misreading Shakespeare or Donne, however. We have the text before us, and may examine at leisure the poet's devices for setting tone.

Finally, another type of muting is that required by historical changes in the meaning of words. We have a tendency to think irrelevantly of a cabbage or pumpkin when Marvell's "vegetable love" is mentioned. Our only justification for reading exclusively modern meanings into Donne, occurs when we may in so doing help reconstruct the actual tone of a passage—and even then we must be sure to distinguish between the old and the new meanings. In "Elegie XVI," Frenchmen are described as "Spittles of diseases." Even if we thought immediately of hospitals, as Donne's audience probably did, we would miss the intended effect. Hospitals no longer symbolize filthiness, for us, but spittle on the sidewalk does. We get the desired effect by thinking in modern terms. (We should, of course, be aware of the process our thinking undergoes.)—The approach I have been advocating in these last few pages, is primarily the historical approach.

# 2

# *Patterns of Parting*

THIS CHAPTER WILL supply, as no other chapter in the essay will, full-length analyses of poems—the type of analyses presupposed by the shorter exegeses elsewhere in the essay. Each atom must be audited, but the full account of the process is reserved for this chapter only.

One may without great violence group Donne's valediction poems together for consideration. Apart from the obvious four (Window, Book, Weeping, Mourning), there are a number of poems which might be classed as valedictions. I have here chosen the Weeping and the Mourning valedictions, plus "Elegie XVI." In each of these three poems the speaker is bidding his beloved farewell, prior to an extended absence. The attitude towards the beloved in these poems, is Petrarchan, rather than cynical. Indeed, their tone is so lovingly tender that these poems have become specifically identified, on the basis of the sinceritas heresy plus somewhat scanty external evidence, with Donne's own biography: he as the model husband must have been addressing his devoted wife.

My choice of these genre poems for this location was not altogether arbitrary (they virtually enjoy genre status). One item of proof is the fact that this group—and the first poem in particular—permits attention to the sinceritas heresy in action. (Here it should be sufficient to say that I am treating the valedictions as dramatic monologues in which the beloved may or may not be the wife of the speaker.) Another item of proof is the fact that the second of the poems supplies *the* classic example of the Metaphysical conceit, while the third poem demonstrates a Metaphysical effect of the type which has no necessary dependence on the figure of speech as such.

T. S. Eliot has listed three Metaphysical effects which Donne (among other poets) employs.[1] First, there is the extended figure of speech which is now commonly referred to as the Metaphysical conceit. Then there is a sort of development by the association of ideas. The third effect is a telescoping of images and associations into a brief but telling phrase: *A bracelet of bright hair about the bone,* for example. The inevitable compass figure of the Mourning valediction illustrates the first type of effect, and the second stanza of the Weeping valediction illustrates the second. (These are Eliot's illustrations.) Before we proceed to the analysis of these two poems, and of a third which provides an example of the third type of effect, we might well examine more of Donne's Metaphysical effects which are not necessarily dependent on the conceit.

Sometimes Donne produces an eerie effect by combining pun with paradox. *Of the Progresse of the Soule* provides an example in lines 45-48:

Thirst for that time [of "God's great *Venite*"], O
      my insatiate soule,
And serve thy thirst, with Gods safe-sealing Bowle.
Be thirstie still, and drinke still till thou goe
To th'only Health, to be Hydroptique so.

The pun on *health* is a favorite with Donne; in the Sermons he refers to Christ's cup as "*salus mundo, a health to all the world."*[2] The poetic version employs a dual paradox with another pun in the balancing element. Two propositions result:

1. Health is illness.
2. Slaking of thirst is constant thirst.

A prose paraphrase would require complexity of statement: In drinking Christ's cup we are drinking a toast to our own well-being, while actually swallowing a healthful draught; the world counts as illness what is the one true health: constant thirst for Christ's cup.

Squeamish readers are sometimes revolted by Donne's choice of imagery. The following reference to Christ on the cross, is something of a test case: "There are those *bowells of compassion*, which are so conspicuous, so manifested, as that you may *see them through his wounds.*"[3] By Donne's time, *bowels of compassion* may or may not have become a dead or even a quiescent metaphor. At any rate, Donne is playing one sense of the phrase against another: a general compassion, perhaps not even localized as visceral, is translated into specific proof of its own authenticity. Christ, that is, has proved his compassion for us, by submitting to wounds for our sake. His gaping side truly reveals his bowels of compassion.—This is no mere cheap pun which holds nothing sacred: it is an insight brought vividly to our attention.

We sometimes feel, in a rather vague way, that Donne's poems progress by the association of ideas. Unfortunately, it is extremely difficult to locate a valid illustration of such a device—Eliot's citation of the Weeping valediction notwithstanding. (See, however, the discussion of lines 27-36 in "Elegie XVIII," Chapter 3, below; and of lines 19-27 in "the Canonization," Chapter 5, below.) One valuable (if predictable) conclusion of Milton A. Rugoff's, in *Donne's Imagery,* might prove useful here. Rugoff notes little essential difference between the verse and the prose imagery of Donne; the verse imagery, however, tends to be elliptical, whereas the prose imagery is more diffuse—and hence easier to follow. If Donne's poems sometimes *do* progress by the association of ideas (and there is certainly thematic repitition of words), the following passage from the Sermons may help to explain the basic functioning of the device:

> . . . Now of this dying Man, that dies in Christ, that dies the Death of the Righteous, that embraces Death as a Sleepe, must wee give you a Picture too.
>
> There is not a minute left to do it; not a minutes sand; Is there a minutes patience? Bee pleased to remember that those Pictures which are deliver'd in a minute, from a print upon a paper, had many dayes, weeks, Moneths time for the graving of those Pictures in the Copper; So this Picture of that dying Man, that dies in Christ, that dies the death of the Righteous, that embraces Death as a Sleepe was graving all his life; All his publique actions were the lights, and all his private the shadowes of this Picture. And when this Picture comes to the Presse, this Man to the streights and agonies of Death, thus he lies, thus he looks, this he is. . . .[4]

Donne had been presenting "two pictures in little; two pictures of dying men; and every man is like one of these, and may know himself by it; he that dies in the Bath of a peaceable, and he that dies upon the wrack of a distracted conscience."[5] The first "picture" is merely a verbal description of the conscience-racked man's approach to death. But notice how the word *Picture* is repeated in the long passage quoted. Our attention is directed to the graphic arts and the relevant implications of the engraving process. Donne's developments of meaning takes this direction (different type faces will be used to show the interlocking continuity): 1. A *picture* is to be given of a man whose DEATH is sleep; 2. not a MINUTE is available for this description (the preacher pretends that his time has run out), or—in another sense—not a MINUTE is available for a running account of the actual dying (death may came unexpectedly); 3. don't be impatient: remember that *pictures* printed in a MINUTE are the product of many months' GRAVING (engraving; preparing for the grave); 4. further substantiation is offered for the picture-death analogy: a. the man's public actions correspond to the unshaded areas of the picture—his private actions, to the shaded portions; b. both man and picture must come to the PRESS (the printing press; "the streights and agonies of Death"—compare the use of "streights" in "Hymne to God my God, in my sicknesse"); 5. the finished product is a faithful *representation.—* This was not a picture *of* the person: the picture *was* the person. Though its logical structure is hardly haphazard, this passage gives an effect like that based on progression by the association of ideas.

One of Donne's effects bears a superficial resemblance to the pathetic fallacy. Consider the eighth stanza of the Window valediction:

> When thy inconsiderate hand
> Flings ope this casement, with my trembling name,
> To looke on one, whose wit or land,
> New battry to thy heart may frame,
> Then thinke this name alive, and that thou thus
> In it offendst my Genius.
> (Ll. 43-48.)

*Trembling* is the key word in this stanza. The speaker of the poem has been ruminating on his name as inscribed on a window-pane of his beloved's chamber. He foresees the time when his mistress will have forgotten him, in his absence. At that time, her hand will be inconsiderate by a kind of conventional metonymy, when she opens her window, to the accomplishment

39

of her lover's "trembling name," to accept the wooing of a new lover. The name trembles because it constitutes a part of the vibrating window, but as a representative of the absent lover, it also trembles for fear of the consequences to his interests. *Trembling,* then, has on the naturalistic level the meaning *vibrating.* On the metaphorical level it means in general terms *pulsing in sympathy* and in specific terms *trembling for fear.*

Even *inconsiderate* has more than one meaning: the lady is not only impetuously careless in throwing the window open, but she is callously indifferent to the anguish she may thus cause her lover, by proxy and ultimately in person.—If this were simply a case of the pathetic fallacy, as it might seem to one fresh from reading Romantic poetry, the sympathetic trembling might have been allocated to a nearby willow, perhaps even if not a breath of air were stirring. In Donne, however, the naturalistic and the symbolic levels are integrated, where a Romantic poet would tend to cut loose from the naturalistic underpinnings.

Francis Thompson, who considered Shelley "To a large extent, . . . what the metaphysical school should have been," has made an interesting distinction between the two types of poetry concerned:

. . . The metaphysical school failed, not because it toyed with imagery, but because it toyed with it frostily. . . . You may toy with imagery in mere intellectual ingenuity, and then you might as well go write acrostics: or you may toy with it in raptures, and then you may write a *Sensitive Plant.* . . .[6]

Most of us would not altogether agree with Thompson, I think—though, in spite of Miss Tuve's elaborate system of qualifications and counter-qualifications, her book leaves one with the impression that Metaphysical imagery is little more than "intellectual ingenuity." Donne seldom "toyed" with imagery in any sense, though we may indicate varying degrees of success in his use of imagery, on the basis of what the imagery does in a poem. In place of Donne's trembling name, in the valediction, we get a mimosa with leaves of hair-trigger sensitivity, to symbolize beauty in Shelley's "The Sensitive Plant."

2

A VALEDICTION: OF WEEPING

Let me powre forth
My teares before thy face, whil'st I stay here,
For thy face coines them, and thy stamps they beare,
And by this Mintage they are something worth,
5      For thus they bee
      Pregnant of thee,
Fruits of much grief they are, emblemes of more,
When a teare falls, that thou falst which it bore,
So thou and I are nothing then, when on a divers shore.

10      On a round ball
A workeman that hath copies by, can lay
An Europe, Afrique, and an Asia,
And quickly make that, which was nothing, *All*,
      So doth each teare,
15      Which thee doth weare,
A globe, yea world by that impression grow,
Till thy teares mixt with mine doe overflow
This world, by waters sent from thee, my heaven dissolved so.

O more then Moone,
20 Draw not up seas to drowne me in thy spheare,
Weepe me not dead, in thine armes, but forbeare
To teach the sea, what it may doe too soone,
      Let not the winde
      Example finde,
25 To doe me more harme, then it purposeth,
Since thou and I sigh one anothers breath,
Who e'r sighes most, is cruellest, and hasts the others death.

This poem is extremely dense in implication of phrasing, but—from my point of view—is none the less unified and uniform in tone. The situation is that of a tearful parting; the implication (dense though it is), merely that absence from one another is unendurable, for lovers. Donne's favorite multiple-choice device is in evidence here. The speaker starts out with the idea that profuse weeping is advantageous: he should endow his tears with value while he may. But tears soon symbolize for him various types of annihilation. Each of the first two stanzas contrasts implied eulogy of the lady with a heightened sense of pain at the nothingness which separation means. By the third stanza the speaker has apparently stopped weeping, himself, and is entreating the lady—to the accompaniment of additional eulogy—to follow his example. Thus they may soften the impact of parting, and salvage whatever is salvageable.

William Empson has devoted a number of pages to a close reading of this poem.[7] My own reading is highly indebted to Empson's, but I still find cause for disagreement: from my point of view, Empson misreads the poem by discovering an ambiguity which does not exist. See the Appendix for a discussion of Empson and the sinceritas heresy, among other things in connection with this poem.

By pouring forth his tears before his lady's face, while he is still present with her, the speaker may give them a currency they lacked before. By reflection the lady's face coins them, imprinting her stamp and thus giving them value. The face coins the tears in the sense that Lincoln's face may be said to coin a penny, but in another sense the sight of the beloved's face coins (i.e., provokes) the tears.

By this process of pouring forth, the tears become pregnant of the lady: their rotundity bears her as in the womb, her presence lends value (as earlier implied; *pregnant of thee* may mean *valuable through your agency*), and each tear's fall pregnantly (significantly, momentously) foreshadows her own. In an obvious sense, the tears are fruits of much grief at the parting, and emblems of more—the devastating effects of separation. When a tear (like a fruit) falls, that entity named *Thou* falls with it. (This interpretation of *thou* [line 8] is based on the reading *falls,* which is found in numerous manuscripts.) The lady falls into nothingness, and the lover is consequently bereft of all being. Both, then, are reduced to nothing, when separated by a sea of salt tears. (If we may think of a *diver's* as well as a *diverse* [e] shore, there may be an implication of paradoxical poverty in wealth: we are nothing in the midst of [but because of] these pearls of great price.—I would hardly insist on this reading, but there may be a support for it in a passage quoted below in connection with line 18. A resemblance between tears and pearls is noted in this passage.)

If, on general principles, one prefers (as I do) the 1633-69 reading of line 8 (*falst*) to the MS. reading *falls,* it is still hardly necessary to postulate a radically different interpretation. The tears are emblems of much grief, and of more: they are emblems of the fact that, when a tear falls, the lady ("thou") who bore it (i.e., caused it to fall or to grow—an extension of the obstetrical and the fruit-tree figures)—or whom it symbolically bore—also falls into nothingness. (Regarding the symbolic bearing of the woman in the tear, such a figure occurs in the lyric of *Love's Labour's Lost,* IV, iii, 26-31.) This, I take it, is basically Empson's interpretation, except that he would combine the two readings of line 8 into a single ambiguity—an impossibility, it seems to me, since neither *falls* nor *falst* can carry, in addition to its own, precisely the syntactical meaning that the other carries (i.e., *thou* considered as merely an entity, requirest a third-person verb). (This, as the Appendix makes evident, is not the non-existent ambiguity I mentioned.)

The second stanza shows, I think, that the *nothing* of the first stanza is used in a qualified sense: a nothing is something which fails to perform its intended function. Such a nothing is a globe which has not yet had the continents laid out upon it; when the process is completed, nothing becomes in a double sense all (i.e., all the world, and all the entity it was intended to be). (There is, of course, the likelihood that the "round ball" was also a nothing because of its cipher-shape.) In like manner, each tear bearing the lady's image becomes first a globe (by the weight of the image's impression), and then a true world (by virtue of the totality of value it encloses). Donne's favorite microcosm figure appears once more.

It is just possible that the lovers' tears may have mingled at the end of the first stanza; the other two stanzas end with a mingling of emotional manifestations. *Bore* in line 8 may refer to weeping—not merely to incitement to weeping. *So* of line 9 might then refer to a similar process on the speaker's part: when his tear falls, he himself falls (the tear is an emblem of the person). In weeping individually, then, on separated shores, the two are individually nothing. All value is lost which does not accrue "whil'st I stay here."

At any rate, the two lovers are weeping in unison by the end of the second stanza. The lovers' miscrocosmic world is flooded "by waters sent from thee" (i.e., tears wept by the lady, plus tears wept at departure from her). The speaker's "heaven" is dissolved in that his lady's image is dissipated, but it is difficult to visualize the cosmic objective correlative, unless we think of Noah's flood plus another Biblical phenomenon: the firmament separating the waters of early creation. There is a pertinent passage in the Sermons: "God made the firmament, which he called heaven, after it had divided the waters: after we have distinguished our tears, natural from spiritual, worldly from heavenly, then there is a firmament established in us, then there is a heaven opened to us: and truly, to cast pearls before swine, will scarce be better resembled [emulated], than to shed tears (which resemble pearls) for worldly losses."[8]—It is possible to maintain, of course, that *my heaven dissolved so* means *in the manner described* ["by waters sent from thee"] *my heaven* [by weeping a cloudburst of tears] *effected dissolution* of itself and the world. (As I have indicated earlier, I do not follow Eliot in considering this stanza particularly representative of Donne's technique of development by the association of ideas.)

The third stanza marks an attempt to salvage something from the destruction which separation imposes. Here the lady is more celestial than a mere moon, but the lunar comparison indicates the power which she may wield. The earth is in a sense her sphere of influence, and she may draw up tides of tears to drown her sublunary lover. In another case, he is within her Ptolemaic sphere (within the "arms" of the moon), and she may drown him either by drawing up seas from the earth to express her grief, or by weeping him dead in a more prosaic manner: he is about to set sail on a perilous voyage; her weeping may encourage the waves, and her sighing the wind, to malevolence even greater than usual.

The implicit reference to sighing becomes explicit in a figure involving mutual exchange of identity: the lovers are sighing with one another's breath; paradoxically, the one who sighs the more is the crueller, not the more loving, since the other's breath is thereby expended more rapidly, and his death accelerated. (According to Renaissance medical philosophy, the vital spirits of the blood were exhausted by excessively frequent breathing or sighing, as well as by excessive evacuation or by corruption of the humors.[9]) The poem ultimately, then, becomes a valediction forbidding mourning.

3

### A VALEDICTION: FORBIDDING MOURNING

As virtuous men passe mildly away
  And whisper to their soules, to goe,
Whilst some of their sad friends doe say,
  The breath goes now, and some say, no:

5 So let us melt, and make no noise,
  No teare-floods, nor sigh-tempests move,
T'were prophanation of our joyes
  To tell the layetie our love.

Moving of th'earth brings harmes and feares,
10  Men reckon what it did and meant,
But trepidation of the spheares,
  Though greater farre, is innocent.

Dull sublunary lovers love
  (Whose soule is sense) cannot admit
15 Absence, because it doth remove
  Those things which elemented it.

But we by a love, so much refin'd,
  That our selves know not what it is,
Inter-assured of the mind,
20  Care lesse, eyes, lips, and hands to misse.

Our two soules therefore, which are one,
  Though I must goe, endure not yet
A breach, but an expansion,
  Like gold to ayery thinnesse beate.

25 If they be two, they are two so
  As stiffe twin compasses are two,
Thy soule the fixt foot, makes no show
  To move, but doth, if the'other doe.

And though it in the center sit,
30  Yet when the other far doth rome,

46

> It leanes, and hearkens after it,
> And growes erect, as that comes home.

> Such wilt thou be to mee, who must
> Like th'other foot, obliquely runne;
35    Thy firmnes makes my circle just,
> And makes me end, where I begunne.

The tone throughout this poem is set by the opening figure, which urges calm acceptance of the situation. There is a certain dignity and sacred genuineness about the love of the speaker and his lady; hence, they are not to protest too much, when destiny decrees separation. There is a disparagement of lovers who *do* make a great fuss over separation; naturally, they are inferior beings whose love depends on physical propinquity.

Here an alternative account of their relationship is introduced. There will really be no separation at all, since their relationship is spiritual, and their souls are one. But a counter-alternative is introduced immediately. If their souls *are* two, they are two only as, etc.—the famous compass figure here graphically representing the close interrelationship between the lovers.

Izaak Walton, in the final edition (1675) of his *Life* of Donne, prints this poem as "a Copy of Verses given by Mr. Donne to his wife at the time that he then [in 1611] parted from her."[10] Modern research has shown that Walton's statements are often highly inaccurate; the fact that this statement was not recorded until long after Donne's death, may cast some doubt upon its accuracy, though we have no external means in this case of checking up on Walton. At any rate, the literary value of the poem is in no way dependent upon its connection with Donne's private life. For the purposes of the poem, a lover—any devoted lover—is addressing his lady, prior to departure on a journey.

The speaker gets to the point immediately, by offering a graphic illustration of his theme. Virtuous men supposedly meet death with noble calmness; instead of holding onto life with desperation, their bodies virtually whisper a release to their souls—with the result that none of the watchers at the bedside can say precisely when death occurs. Parting is nothing to be afraid of, the speaker implicitly reminds his beloved; demonstrative grief would merely give their secret away to the general, and thus profane the sanctity of their love (secular, again, in terms of sacred love). The tear-floods and sigh-tempests of the Weeping valediction, are to be avoided at all costs.

Lines 5 and 6 might be paraphrased in two versions: In the same manner, let us separate, and make no noise in the process—let us stir up neither tear-floods nor sigh-tempests; *or,* . . . let (the temptation to) neither tear-floods nor sigh-tempests move us emotionally.—The emotional implications of the verb *move* are echoed in line 9, "Moving of th'earth brings harmes and feares," where *harmes* may equate *distress.* The precise meaning of *Moving of th'earth* is in question. Charles M. Coffin has made out a case for a contrast here between the "old" and the "new philosophy."[11] One may contend, however, that the motion in question is not that of the earth as a planet, but rather that of a seismic upheaval. Earthquakes bring damage (which men proceed to estimate); earthquakes bring fears—including the fear of God (men speculate upon divine fury). All this disturbance, however, affects only a small segment of the earth, whereas trepidation of the spheres, an eccentric movement on a cosmic scale, is imperceptible (in any direct way) to the human individual. (*Trepidation* is a term from Ptolemaic astronomy, as revised; by postulating a ninth sphere as the cause of eccentric movements, it supposedly accounts for such phenomena as precession of the equinoxes.) The application (if not the precise meaning) of this technical language, is not at all obscure: The really important events are unheralded by fanfare and unattended by terrors.

The fourth stanza describes the type of lovers who *should* quake at the thought of parting. A term from the old astronomy is used to characterize them: they are "sublunary lovers"—i. e., prosaically ordinary humans whose love has not mounted beyond the sphere of the moon, to the upper ethereal regions. *Sublunary* conveys a sense of being under the moon's sway, and hence inconstant or even lunatic. Lovers of this type belong to the laity who lack reverence for love's mysteries. Sensuality (or at least sensuousness) being the essence of their love, absence destroys love by removing its component elements—i.e., the "eyes, lips, and hands" of line 20.—Donald A. Stauffer, discussing metrical effects in this poem, cites an "etymological pun" on *Absence* (line 15) which would demonstrate that both syllables were to be stressed rhetorically.[12] Stauffer's meaning, I suppose, is that sublunary lovers (whose soul is *sense*), cannot admit *ab-sence* [-*sense*]. This pun quite likely occurs; cf. the name of Abhorson, the executioner in *Measure for Measure*. In both cases, the *Ab* element would have the value of the Latin preposition; *Absence* and *Abhorson* would then equate respectively *Departure-from-sense* and *Son-of-a-bitch*.

But the speaker and his beloved possess a different type of love, so refined as to elude all analysis. They receive mutual assurances of love through the mind, and hence their spiritual relationship is well-nigh independent of "sense" and undaunted by distance.

Since the refinement of their love extends to their souls, the two souls (made one by love) are capable of expanding indefinitely without bursting asunder, and the effect is likened to that possible with extremely thin gold foil.

But in a sense the souls *are* still two, just as the legs of a draftsman's compass are two. From Dr. Johnson to John Crowe Ransom, this particular figure has been cited to demonstrate Metaphysical technique. While it illustrates rather aptly Donne's typical wedding of worlds—in this case, the worlds of love and draftsmanship—we should be wary of calling it a typical figure so far as point-to-point correspondences between tenor and vehicle are concerned. In other cases the correspondency may be much greater or much less, though we may say in general that Donne's "imagery" seldom lends itself readily to visualization.

In this well-known figure the fixed foot of the compass literally moves (rotates on a fixed point, in varying angles of erectness) when the other foot moves, but the figurative movement of the fixed foot must be merely emotion or empathy, prior to the leaning and erectness which signify hearkening and welcome. (*Show/To move,* I think, hearkens back to the poem's basic injunction against demonstrative parting.) Again, the roaming amounts to mere widening of radius, since all points on each circle drawn are equidistant from the fixed foot. Yet the implication of the last stanza is that the completion of a "just" circle "makes me end where I begun" (reunited with the beloved). The adverb *obliquely* is not immediately visualizable in terms of the lovers' spatial relationship; the sense is one of controlled-askew movement or of obligatory deviation from a fixed track—figuratively, enforced absence from the beloved.— But the basic theme of this valediction is that the parting is merely illusory: the death-of-absence never occurs, and weeping would be superfluous here.

## 4

### ELEGIE XVI

#### ON HIS MISTRIS

By our first strange and fatall interview,
By all desires which thereof did ensue,
By our long starvling hopes, by that remorse
Which my words masculine perswasive force

5    Begot in thee, and by the memory
      Of hurts, which spies and rivals threatened me,
      I calmly beg: But by thy Parents wrath,
      By all paines, which want and divorcement hath,
      I conjure thee, and all the oathes which I
10   And thou have sworne to seale joynt constancy,
      Here I unsweare, and overswear them thus,
      Thou shalt not love by means so dangerous.
      Temper, O faire Love, loves impetuous rage,
      Be my true Mistris still, not my faign'd Page;
15   I'll goe, and, by thy kinde leave, leave behinde
      Thee, onely worthy to nurse in my minde,
      Thirst to come backe; O if thou die before,
      From other lands my soule towards thee shall soare.
      Thy (else Almighty) beautie cannot move
20   Rage from the Seas, nor thy love teach them love,
      Nor tame wilde Boreas harshnesse; Thou hast reade
      How roughly hee in pieces shivered
      Faire Orithea, whom he swore he lov'd.
      Fall ill or good, 'tis madnesse to have prov'd
25   Dangers unurg'd; Feed on this flattery,
      That absent Lovers one in th'other be.
      Dissemble nothing, not a boy, nor change
      Thy bodies habite, nor mindes; bee not strange
      To thy selfe onely; All will spie in thy face
30   A blushing womanly discovering grace;
      Richly cloath'd Apes, are call'd Apes, and as soone
      Ecclips'd as bright we call the Moone the Moone.
      Men of France, changeable Camelions,
      Spittles of diseases, shops of fashions,
35   Lyves fuellers, and the rightest company
      Of Players, which upon the worlds stage be,
      Will quickly know thee, and know thee, alas!
      Th'indifferent Italian, as we passe
      His warme land, well content to thinke thee Page,
40   Will hunt thee with such lust, and hideous rage,
      As *Lots* faire guests were vext. But none of these
      Nor spungy hydroptique Dutch shall thee displease,
      If thou say here. O stay here, for, for thee

England is onely a worthy Gallerie,
45 To walke in expectation, till from thence
Our greatest King call thee to his presence.
When I am gone, dreame me some happinesse,
Nor let thy lookes our long hid love confesse,
Nor praise, nor dispraise me; Bless nor curse
50 Openly loves force, nor in bed fright thy Nurse
With midnights startings, crying out, oh, oh
Nurse, O my love is slaine, I saw him goe
O'r the white Alpes alone; I saw him I,
Assail'd, fight, taken, stabb'd, bleed, fall, and die.
55 Augure me better chance, except dread *Jove*
Thinke it enough for me to'have had thy love.

In tone this poem combines in a curious mixture the tenderness of "Sweetst love," for example, with the unexpurgated
realism of the Satyres. Devoted, and considerate of his lady's
welfare, the speaker realistically advises her against braving the
elements (among other dangers) to accompany him on a trip:
the elements, after all, will fail to recognize the sovereignty of
her beauty. A candid passage on the sexual molestation she may
encounter, is followed by a reference to her present state—peace-
fully residing in England as in the ante-chamber of Heaven.
After a vivid passage describing the harm she can do him by
forebodings of bad luck, the speaker implies that even such a
fate cannot outweigh his good fortune as a recipient of her love.
—Throughout the poem there is a nice balance of eulogy and
tenderness, with realism and common sense.

Though thematically it covers several of the points we have
found in the other valedictions, this poem belongs almost to a
different poetic genre—with the combination we have noted,
here, of Petrarchan adoration and vividly described satirical
scenes from real life. In the canon, of course, it *does* fall under
the Elegies, rather than under the Songs and Sonets (like the
other valedictions we have considered). As will be noted in

Chapter 3, below, the specialized funereal or nostalgic overtones of the term *elegy* mark a comparatively modern development. In the classical tradition an elegy was a poem written in
elegiac metre and dealing with such subjects as love and war.

As Grierson reminds us, practically nothing was too fantastic
to happen in real life in Elizabethan times. Here we find a lover
dissuading his lady from her plan to accompany him, disguised
as a page, on a journey he is about to take. At least two stock
valediction-notions are expressed: "That absent Lovers one in
th'other be"; and that destiny may carry out pessimistic forebodings. These notions, however, are used uniquely within the
context of this poem.

Grierson is notable in his printed text of the poem, for lack-
ing the courage of his convictions. In certain cases he finds the
manuscript readings definitely superior to those of the editions,
yet he still prints the version of the latter. (This poem was first
printed in the 1635 edition; Grierson's experience indicates
that, in such cases, manuscript readings are often to be preferred
to those of the editions; see Grierson, I, vi.) Grierson postulates
an editorial revision in line 7 to help make the poem fit Donne's
biography, one in line 37 to bowdlerize a "radical want of deli-
cacy," and one in line 49 to make the metre more mellifluous.
I am inclined to agree and to modify the text accordingly.
Indeed—in the absence of any conclusive evidence in the favor
of the editions—where the editions and the MSS. diverge, I have
adopted MS. readings—even in line 35, where Grierson considers the 1635 reading clearly superior. (Far from attempting
to supplant Grierson, I am assuming that any reader skeptical
of my conclusions will have Grierson close at hand. Grierson's
wealth of information is basic, and will continue to be so.)

The speaker begins his argument by recalling the many
dangers and hardships he and his lady have endured in the name
of love. Their first sight of one another ("interview") was

strange in that neither had seen the like of the other before; it was fatal in the sense that their fates were thenceforth joined, but also fatal in view of the painful difficulties which followed. Also invoked are the desires aroused by this meeting, their long-deferred fulfillment, the remorse which the lady experienced on yielding to his importunities, and the memory of threats from his rivals and from spies sent to watch their actions together. A new series begins here with the lady's being entreated by the (potential?) wrath of her parents and by the hardships resulting from separation and its disadvantages.

Rather than have her endure such hardships again, the lover is willing to release her from their bonds of fidelity. He unswears these oaths and supersedes them, all in one forceful asseveration: "Thou shalt not love by means so dangerous." She is to remain his mistress, rather than become his feigned page. *True* and *faign'd* supply the implication: Being my mistress is your true vocation in life.—But there is also an allusion to fidelity in *true*.

It is interesting to note, here, Donne's use of semi-quiescent metaphors. In lines 3-5, the speaker's words are described as having exerted a "masculine perswasive force" to beget remorse in the lady; the metaphor is saved from total abstraction on the one hand and mixed status on the other, by the subject matter's implicit reference to intercourse. Whether or not conception occurred in the physiological sense, remorse was begotten by the act—and hence, indirectly, by the words. Lines 16f. contain a somewhat similar effect; the lady is to nurse, in her lover's mind, the thirst to return. Translated into relatively neutral terms, the statement means that she is to arouse and encourage in him the desire to return (and she alone is worth the trip back). But there is also an implicit allusion to the suckling of infants; the thought of being with her again—and nothing but that thought—is capable of slaking (while arousing) his thirst to return.

The lover insists on being realistic about the power of his lady's beauty, which "cannot move/Rage from the Seas"—i. e., can neither influence the seas' rage, nor remove it. Nor can her beauty tame the wild wind; in one of his rare allusions to classical mythology, Donne cites the case of Boreas, who raped the nymph Orithyia—look how rough his treatment of her was, despite his protestations of love. In short, the lady would be mad, to ask for trouble and undergo dangers needlessly.

*Flattery* is the name given here to the notion that absent lovers exchange identities. There is an interesting parallel to this passage in the final couplet of Shakespeare's "Sonnet 42." Shakespeare (or the dramatic *I*) is deriving what comfort he can from the thought that his friend is stealing his mistress from him:

> But here's the joy, my friend and I are one,
> Sweete flattery, then she loves but me alone.

In both contexts, *flattery* seems to mean *sophistry which is gratefully to be received, if not swallowed.* Donne's speaker may mean, then: Be content with this casuistry—that you will be present with me anyway, in male form.—The lady is to change neither her body's habit (clothing) nor the habit of her mind; she would fool nobody but herself. Her feminine charm would give her away immediately, since she is no more capable of disguise than an ape or the moon. (Notice the natural tone of the vehicle in this implied figure of speech; comparison with the moon might be not unflattering, but the ape connotations plainly do not belong to the lady here. In this connection, see Chapter 1, above.) The speaker then enumerates the hazards she would encounter on the Continent. Frenchmen are veritable

55

hospitals of disease; for the sanitation-conscious modern, at least, *Spittles* has an additional concreteness. But there are richer puns in this passage on Frenchmen.

For some reason I have been unable to discover, Grierson considers the MS. reading *Lyves fuellers* in line 35 as "very remarkable." Indeed, if he had been convinced of its correctness, he would have preferred the MS. readings throughout. Though I am unaware of its mystic significance, I *do* consider this reading correct, since it can include the meaning of the 1635 edition (*Loves fuellers*) and provide a meaning of its own. As love's fuellers, the Frenchmen would be exponents of aphrodisiacs, for example, or experimenters in new erotic thrills (they are most justly entitled to the name of *Players*); as life's fuellers, they would incidentally keep the birth-rate high. (In certain words, *f* between vowels became[v]; hence *Lyves* instead of *Lyfes*. Cf. the etymology of *alive* in the *NED*.) Phonetically, *Lyves* would have probably been pronounced something like [lʌɪvz]—superficially similar to the conjectural pronunciation of *Loves* at that time.[13]

I have based my reading of line 37 on that of a single manuscript, the Stephens MS. at Harvard—the only one which seems to have escaped clerical "improvement" in the transmission of this particular line. There are several manuscripts, however, which (from my point of view) record only one excrescent word. The 1635 reading provides for no ambiguities at all, and the MSS. I have mentioned provide for only one, but the single MS. I have chosen, provides for a double-ambiguity characteristic of Donne: The Frenchmen "Will quickly know thee, and know thee, alas!" That is, they will quickly know the lady [recognize her as] a lass, and will immediately know her [carnally], alas!

Italians are depicted as indifferently heterosexual or homosexual. They will gladly accept the lady as an attractive young boy, and will pursue her with the lust of Lot's townspeople toward his angelic guests (see Genesis 19). Fools rush in where angels fear to tread. The reference to the Dutch as "spungy" and "hydroptique" (extremely thirsty) may involve a tongue-in-cheek allusion to bucco-lingual practices, which might seem natural to inhabitants of the *nether* lands (cf. *The Comedy of Errors*, III, ii); it may, however, simply refer to misbehavior in drunkenness (cf. *spongy* in *Macbeth*, I, vii, 71; *spunginess* in *Sermon XXI* of *Fifty Sermons;*[14] and *hydroptique* in "Holy Sonnet III," line 9).

But all these hazards can be avoided if the lady stays at home. England may be for her an entrance hall, an ante-chamber to God's throneroom. In his absence she is to "dreame me some happinesse," but to conceal all signs of their "long hid love." The two seemingly disparate injunctions combine in an example of what, above all, she is not to do—reveal their love in a nightmare outburst prompted by a vision of his violent death. "Augure me better chance," he pleads. But then it occurs to him that even such a fate is not too harsh for one who has enjoyed her love..

There is an odd quality in the imagery of the nightmare passage. The image impression is eminently visualizable—the murder of a traveler passing "O'r the white Alpes alone." It has the weirdly symbolic tone of Ernest Hemingway's "The Snows of Kilimanjaro." In fact, it is even possible that this very passage suggested, to the pre-bell-tolling Hemingway, the symbol of death as a bleak and snow-clad mountain.

## 3

# *Off With That Girdle!*

THIS CHAPTER IS concerned with the matter of sensuous imagery in Donne. The poems to be analyzed here are "Elegie XVIII," "Elegie XIX," and the Valentine epithalamium—possibly Donne's nearest approach to Spenser in the field of sensuous imagery. It so happens that all three poems are concerned, in situation, with physical love. For that reason the title of this chapter may not be inappropriate. Someone may object that *Girdle* here has for the reader a modern, not a 17 c., sense. Quite true, but the context of the phrase in "Elegie XIX" leads us to believe that the phrase-meaning (if not the word-meaning) had the same force for Donne's contemporaries that it now has for us.

In his book on Donne's imagery, Rugoff notes the relative scarcity of images drawn directly from the senses, and concludes that too much attention has been paid to the language of the senses in Donne. Has Rugoff been betrayed by statistics? Or is Eliot's famous dictum (" . . . a direct sensuous apprehension of thought. . . .") the product of a snap judgment?—In his review of Rugoff's book, George Williamson has an interesting comment on this matter: "When we are told that the number of images which issue from the direct experience of the senses is negligible in Donne (p. 227), we want to know why Donne was ever called sensual, or why any stomachs were ever queasy over the 'Elegies.' Mr. Rugoff, in fact, is so preoccupied with the intellectual aspects of Donne's imagery that we are likely to get the impression not only that his imagery is defecated of all substance, but that his abstractions are not highly energized shadows."[1]

Williamson's choice of *sensual* is not a particularly happy one. Much of Donne is sensual in subject matter without being notably sensuous in imagery. We might say that Donne is at the opposite pole from Spenser, who—while extolling the virtues—paints pictures of such rich sensuous detail as to incite the impressionable to evil.—Perhaps a comparison with Herrick would be more just, however. We might compare passages from the two with sensual subject matter in common, but with opposite stress on the elements of wit and sensuousness. Donne's "Elegie XVIII" refers to "the streight *Hellespont* betweene/The *Sestos* and *Abydos* of [a lady's] breasts,/ (Not of two Lovers, but two Loves the neasts). . . ." The breasts here represent—not the home towns of Hero and Leander—but the focal point of two types of love: maternal and erotic. Though the context is sensual, the image is primarily intellectual in appeal. (The geographical analogy eventually leads, of course, to an unmistakably erotic region.)—Herrick's "Fresh Cheese and Cream" is rather different:

> Would ye have fresh cheese and cream?
> Julia's breast can give you them:
> And, if more, each nipple cries:
> To your cream here's strawberries.[2]

The element of wit is attenuated here, but the sensuous appeal is vivid.—These are somewhat extreme examples, of course, but they point up a basic contrast.

As we have noted earlier, it is not always easy to determine the number of congruent points between the tenor and the vehicle of a metaphor in Donne. If there is close relationship between the two in the following passage from "Epithalamion," the sensuous element is unusually strong here:

> As he that sees a starre fall, runs apace,
>   And finds a gellie in the place,
>     So doth the Bridegroome hast as much,
> Being told this starre is falne, and finds her such.
>
> (Ll. 204-207.)

This is actually a simile—not a metaphor—of course.

There *are* indisputably sensuous passages in Donne, apart from those in the erotic Elegies and the Epithalamions. They are not necessarily found in sensual contexts. One such passage appears in *The Progresse of the Soule*:

> Outcrept a sparrow, this soules moving Inne,
> On whose raw armes stiffe feathers now begin,
> As childrens teeth through gummes, to breake with
>       paine,
> His flesh is jelly yet, and his bones threds,
> All a new downy mantle overspreads,
> A mouth he opes, which would as much containe
> As his late house, and the first houre speaks plaine,
> And chirps alowd for meat. Meat fit for men
> His father steales for him, and so feeds then
>       One, that within a moneth, will beate him from
>             his hen.
>
> (Ll. 181-190.)

Such extended naturalitic description is somewhat rare in Donne, however, though his diction is invariably precise and concrete—even when his imagery is primarily intellectual.

We might well turn, here, to Eliot's comment on the language of the senses (to adapt Wordsworth's phrase). Eliot refers to "a direct sensuous apprehension of thought, or a re-creation of thought into feeling."[3]

... Tennyson and Browning are poets, and they think; but they do not feel their thought as immediately as the odour of a rose. A thought to Donne was an experience; it modified his sensibility. When a poet's mind is perfectly equipped for its work, it is constantly amalgamating disparate experience; the ordinary man's experience is chaotic, irregular, fragmentary. The latter falls in love, or reads Spinoza, and these two experiences have nothing to do with each other, or with the noise of the typewriter or the smell of cooking; in the mind of the poet these experiences are always forming new wholes.[4]

Elsewhere Eliot notes that for Donne " thought is an intense feeling which is one with every other feeling."[5]

It should be evident that Eliot's "sensuous" is an adjective far more applicable to Donne or the Symbolistes than it is to Spenser (however unjustly the former Elizabethan has been exalted of late at the latter's expense). S. L. Bethell has an interesting reworking of Eliot's comment:

... Donne's poems are not reflections done into verse; they are truly acts of the mind: we feel that he is analysing and organising his experience as he writes and his last line rounds off and signalizes a simultaneous achievement of thought. Feelings may be his subject-matter and his thinking passionate, but it is undoubtedly the intellect that predominates—not, of course, the skeleton Reason of the eighteenth century but the intellect which is the full man energetically confronting experience. ...[6]

If Donne enjoyed thought as if it were sense-perception, perhaps we should preface our analyses of "Elegie XVIII," etc., with a brief look at a somewhat more typical poem in Donne. In the "Hymne to God my God, in my sicknesse," discovery of an intellectual (though also emotional) fact, is put on the same level with physical exploration and discovery. The poem turns on the semantic implications of *straits,* with the imagery centering around this concept. Donne as poet specializes in discovering the relatedness of things; his "South-west discoverie" here is the fact that straits and only straits—in human existence as well as in geography—lead to the coveted treasure-lands. The predicaments (straits) of our experience may paradoxically represent God's blessing. Donne is dying *"Per fretum febris, by these streights"*—hard by the straits of fever he has just succeeded in discovering, but also by (through the agency of) fever's raging. ". . . In his purple wrapp'd," Donne begs, "receive me Lord,/By these his thornes give me his other Crowne. . . ." The two requests are parallel: By my token participation—as a mortal, suffering death—in the passion of Christ (his crown of thorns; the mock robes of royalty and the "purple" blood lacing his body), exalt me in proportion to my passion ( give me the crown and the purple robes of royalty).—As Grierson points out, Donne puts much the same idea into his own epitaph, with Christian emphasis on his favorite terms of the phoenix and the meeting of East and West. Donne the Renaissance explorer has made a great discovery: the Occident and the Orient actually meet, and their meeting-place is the nest of the phoenix.

HIC LICET IN  OCCIDVO CINERE ASPICIT EVM
CVJVS NOMEN EST ORIENS.

2

### Elegie XVIII
#### Loves Progress

Who ever loves, if he do not propose
The right true end of love, he's one that goes
To sea for nothing but to make him sick:
Love is a bear-whelp born, if we o're lick

Our love, and force it new strange shapes to take,
We erre, and of a lump a monster make.
Were not a Calf a monster that were grown
Face'd like a man, though better then his own?
Perfection is in unitie: preferr
One woman first, and then one thing in her.
I, when I value gold, may think upon
The ductilness, the application,
The wholsomness, the ingenuitie,
From rust, from soil, from fire ever free:
But if I love it, 'tis because 'tis made
By our new nature (use) the soul of trade.
     All these in women we might think upon
(If women had them) and yet love but one.
Can men more injure women then to say
They love them for that, by which they're not they?
Makes virtue woman? must I cool my bloud
Till I both be, and find one wise and good?
May barren Angels love so. But if we
Make love to woman; virtue is not she:
As beauty'is not nor wealth: He that strayes thus
From her to hers, is more adulterous,
Then if he took her maid. Search every spheare
And firmament, our *Cupid* is not there:
He's an infernal god and under ground,
With *Pluto* dwells, where gold and fire abound:
Men to such Gods, their sacrificing Coles
Did not in Altars lay, but pits and holes.
Although we see Celestial bodies move
Above the earth, the earth we Till and love:
So we her ayres contemplate, words and heart,
And virtues; but we love the Centrique part.
     Nor is the soul more worthy, or more fit
For love, then this, as infinite as it.
But in attaining this desired place
How much they erre; that set out at the face?
The hair a Forest is of Ambushes,
Of springes, snares, fetters and manacles:
The brow becalms us when 'tis smooth and plain,

And when 'tis wrinckled, shipwracks us again.
45   Smooth, 'tis a Paradice, where we would have
Immortal stay, and wrinkled 'tis our grave.
The Nose (like to the first Meridian) runs
Not 'twixt an East and West, but 'twixt two suns;
It leaves a Cheek, a rosie Hemisphere
50   On either side, and then directs us where
Upon the Islands fortunate we fall,
(Not faynte *Canaries,* but *Ambrosiall*)
Her swelling lips; To which when wee are come,
We anchor there, and think our selves at home,
55   For they seem all: there Syrens songs, and there
Wise Delphick Oracles do fill the ear;
There in a Creek where chosen pearls do swell,
The Remora, her cleaving tongue doth dwell.
These, and the glorious Promontory, her Chin
60   Ore past; and the streight *Hellespont* betweene
The *Sestos* and *Abydos* of her breasts,
(Not of two Lovers, but two Loves the neasts)
Succeeds a boundless sea, but yet thine eye
Some Island moles may scattered there descry;
65   And sailing towards her *India,* in that way
Shall at her fair Atlantick Navell stay;
Though thence the Current be thy Pilot made,
Yet ere thou be where thou wouldst be embay'd,
Thou shalt upon another Forest set,
70   Where many Shipwrack, and no further get.
When thou are there, consider what this chace
Mispent by thy beginning at the face.
      Rather set out below; practice my Art,
Some Symetry the foot hath with that part
75   Which thou dost see, and is thy Map for that
Lovely enough to stop, but not stay at:
Least subject to disguise and change it is;
Men say the Devil never can change his.
It is the Emblem that hath figured
80   Firmness; 'tis the first part that comes to bed.
Civilitie we see refin'd: the kiss
Which at the face began, transplanted is,

Since to the hand, since to the Imperial knee,
Now at the Papal foot delights to be:
85 If Kings think that the nearer way, and do
Rise from the foot, Lovers may do so too:
For as free Spheres move faster far then can
Birds, whom the air resists, so may that man
Which goes this empty and Aetherial way,
90 Then if at beauties elements he stay.
Rich Nature hath in women wisely made
Two purses, and their mouths aversely laid:
They then, which to the lower tribute owe,
That way which that Exchequer looks, must go:
95 He which doth not, his error is as great,
As who by Clyster gave the Stomack meat.


*Progress,* in the title of this poem, is used in the sense of
*Journey* or *expedition.* In tone the poem is naturalistic, though
not completely so. The assumption is that women have only a
single proper function, and that the sensible male lover will
head directly towards the scene of action, avoiding all diversions
from his course. Oddly enough, objects of Petrarchan adoration
(hair, brow, etc.) are considered formidable diversions—this
fact being a lapse from naturalism.

We are given to understand that non-sensual love is non-
sensical. It is a veritable monstrosity. This poem takes the extreme view, where "The Primrose" (without being any too
complimentary) chose the mean:

For should my true-Love lesse then woman bee,
She were scarce any thing; and then, should she
Be more then woman, shee would get above
　　All thought of sexe, and thinke to move
　　My heart to study her, and not to love;
Both these were monsters . . . .

Ll. 13-18.)

The casuistical argument deals in statements which would seem highly respectable out of context: "Perfection is in unitie"; "He that strayes. . ./From her to hers, is more adulterous,/Then if he took her maid." If we believe in unity, we "preferr one woman" —a respectable argument for monogamy? No, we continue the process and prefer one thing in her: her private parts.

Along similar lines, to love a woman for her wealth or her beauty—not for herself—might figuratively be considered grave adultery. But virtue is classified here with wealth and beauty; they are equally extraneous to woman's basic nature. Cupid is an infernal god who demands that sacrifices to him be buried in "pits and holes." The continuity here is tricky and involved:

1. Cupid is not to be found in the firmament, but— rather—beneath the ground.
2. Tribute must be consequently be paid to the earth.
3. We may view the firmament, but we cultivate the earth.
4. In like manner, we observe a woman's "ayres," etc.— her peripheral atmosphere—but make love to the accessible "Centrique part."

Throughout this poem, the sexual symbolism runs very close to Freud. "Pits and holes" have obvious implications; buried treasure may thus have associations with the female genitalia. Even the foot may have, by transference, a certain symbolic function. Dream symbolism often substitutes the mouth for the female organ. And the "Forest" seems straight out of Freud: in dreams the pubic hairs often masquerade as woods and thickets.[7]—By this reference to Freud I mean to imply—not that Donne's symbolism is out of his conscious control—but that by an intuitive anticipation of Freud, Donne makes his imagery here more functional than we may realize at first.

Part of the structure of this poem—it is somewhat loose, to be sure—depends on recurring use of the buried-treasure theme. It first crops up with reference to gold: we are primarily interested in gold because it is the medium of trade. The application of this statement to women, is no more than oblique. With reference to Cupid's offerings—to be made in the land of gold and fire, pits and holes—the implication is clearer. In geographical terms, love's expedition begins (the long way) somewhere east of the Hellespont, and ends at the mineral wealth of the West Indies. And the penultimate image of the poem is that of two purses which "Rich Nature" has fashioned with "their mouths aversely laid."

> They then, which to the lower tribute owe,
> That way which that Exchequer looks, must go. . . .
> (Ll. 93 f.)

The geographical analogy is of a type familiar to us from *The Comedy of Errors;* as we have seen in Chapter 2, the same type may possibly exist in "Elegie XVI." Even in its upper manifestation, the hair is spoken of as a forest—of snares and fetters which evidently represent clasps for the coiffure, as well as the ineffable qualities which might distract the lover from his true goal. East of the Hellespont, the geographical whereabouts are extremely vague. The "fair Atlantick Navell," however is an ingenious touch; it conveys the idea of a naval base situated (at Gibraltar?) on the earth's rotundity.

The lower route is recommended because it offers fewer distractions—as an "empty . . . way"—and because "Some Symetry the foot hath with that part/Which thou dost seek. . . ." *Symetry* may or may not bear any relationship to shape. Apart from the cleavage of the toes, the foot is hardly a shape-symbol for the female genitalia, though the shoe is quite standard in this connection. At any rate, *Symetry* definitely means *congruity* or *consonance.* The following lines indicate points of similarity, but there may be an additional sense in which the foot serves as map pointing the way to the more desirable part. In *Henry V* we find Katherine denouncing the English words *foot* and *coun* (her attendant's mispronunciation of *gown*) as "mots de son mauvais, corruptible, gros, et impudique, et non pour les dames d'honneur d'user. . . ." (III, iv.) Katherine is thinking of the French *foutre* (to copulate with) and *con* (pudendum).[8] In the performance of the play, *foot* and *coun* were doubtless pronounced with the French vowels—not particularly close to the English—but this fact need not contra-indicate an obscene allusion of this type in Donne, since the French reaction to *foot* may well have been a standing joke of the times. (*Fouter* [*foutre*] appears in *Tristram Shandy,* in the diverting anecdote of the abbess of Andoüillets and the stubborn mules.[9])

Certain points of similarity are definitely stated, however. Both parts of the body are "Least subject to disguise and change" —a reference to the Devil's cloven hoof as a dead giveaway, regardless of his disguise. Each "is the Emblem that hath figured/Firmness. . . ." That is, the foot symbolizes resolute determination (putting one's foot down); the pudendum prefigures (foreshadows) a different kind of firmness: it sets ' our flesh upright" (to borrow a phrase from "Elegie XIX"). And each is "the first part that comes to bed." *Comes* obviously has a sexual implication here.[10] With reference to the pudendum, *to bed* equals *in bed*. The *NED* has a pertinent quotation of this usage: "1658 in Morris *Troub. Cath. Foref.* I. vi (1872) 314 Sister Cornelia who had lain to bed about thirty years."

"He which doth not [pay tribute in the appropriate manner to the lower Exchequer], his error is as great,/As who by Clyster gave the Stomack meat." A clyster is an enema or similar injection. The idea of nutritive clysters is by no means a fantastic product of Donne's imagination; the value of such clysters was a moot question in Renaissance medicine.[11] Whatever his personal belief on the matter, Donne is taking the side of the question which.gives him imaginative support. Paying tribute to

the uncharacteristic facet of women—the statement runs here—
is as absurd as attempting to force food into the part of the
body where waste is normally expelled. The effect is that of the
crude anecdote about the little boy confused by the trunk at his
first sight of an elephant feeding. "You wouldn't believe me if
I told you what he did with his tail."

"Elegie XVIII" is very strong medicine. It is concerned with
physical love, like many of the secular-love poems; it is concerned specifically with the female anatomy, like relatively few
of that number; but its imagery is still virtually as intellectual
in appeal as it is sensuous. The reader who cannot stomach the
imagery in its crude implications, will hardly consider the poem
a success—but neither will the reader who cannot appreciate the
play of wit in the extended geographical metaphor. In the remaining poems of this chapter, we shall find abundant emphasis
on the flesh, but the savage scurrility is absent, and in its place
we find a richer sensuousness.


3

Elegie XIX
Going to Bed

Come, Madam, all rest my powers defie,
Until I labour, I in labour lie.
The foe oft-times having the foe in sight,
Is tir'd with standing though he never fight.
5    Off with that girdle, like heavens Zone glittering,
But a far fairer world incompassing.
Unpin that spangled breastplate which you wear,
That th'eyes of busie fooles may be stopt there,
Unlace your self, for that harmonious chyme,
10    Tells me from you, that now it is bed time.
Off with that happy busk, which I envie
That still can be, and still can stand so nigh.
Your gown going off, such beautious state reveals,

As when from flowry meads th'hills shadow steales.
15   Off with that wyerie Coronet and shew
The haiery Diademe which on you doth grow:
Now off with those shooes, and then safely tread
In this loves hallow'd temple, this soft bed.
In such white robes, heaven's Angels us'd to be
20   Receavd by men; Thou Angel bringst with thee
A heaven like Mahomets Paradise; and though
Ill spirits walk in white, we easily know,
By this these Angels from an evil sprite,
Those set our hairs, but these our flesh upright.
25    License my roaving hands, and let them go,
Before, behind, between above, below.
O my America! my new-found-land,
My kingdome, safliest when with on man man'd,
My Myne of precious stones, My Emperie,
30   How blest am I in this discovering thee!
To enter in these bonds, is to be free;
Then where my hand is set, my seal shall be.
    Full nakedness! All joyes are due to thee,
As soules unbodied, bodies uncloth'd must be,
35   To taste whole joyes. Gems which you women use
Are like Atlanta's balls, cast in mens views,
That when a fools eye lighteth on a Gem,
His earthly soul may covet theirs, not them.
Like pictures, or like books gay coverings made
40   For lay-men, are all women thus array'd;
Themselves are mystick books, which only wee
(Whom their imputed grace will dignifie)
Must see reveal'd. Then since that I may know;
As liberally, as to a Midwife, shew
45   Thy self: cast all, yea, this white lynnen hence,
There is no pennance due to innocence.
    To teach thee, I am naked first; why than
What needst thou have more covering then a man.

The major part of this poem is dedicated to an unblushing
voluptuousness. In this section of the poem there are ambiguities

which contribute richness to the sensuous tone, but the real difficulty of the poem is not primarily verbal, insofar as layers of meaning are concerned. The obscure section (lines 33-45, approximately) consists in tightly-knit reasoning which is rather hard to unravel, but which obviously generates the philosophy on which the rest of the poem operates.

By way of transition from the earlier part of the poem, the virtues of full nakedness are extolled. This type of clothing imagery is a favorite of Donne's. Undiluted spiritual joy can occur only when the soul is fully naked—i. e., stripped of the body—and a like principle applies to joys of the body. We have here the same distinction which is pointed up—however casuistically—in "Elegie XVIII": the difference between essential and accessory traits in women. The female race is depicted as testing men deliberately by dressing in outward finery and noting the men's reactions. Apparently the fools will give themselves away by coveting "theirs, not them." The finery is for outsiders—laymen ignorant of love's esoteric rites; the women themselves are cabalistic books which only the elect "Must see reveal'd." And the speaker is obviously among the elect.

The basic assumption in this poem, then, is related to—but different from—that of "Elegie XVIII." There is no insistence here on the supremacy of the pudendum, but the naked body is exalted, and the implication is that all men are blind to its virtues, except the privileged few specifically enlightened by the mystic society. The distractions from the true good are here evidently—not objects of Petrarchan adoration, as in the preceding elegy—but objects or symbols of material wealth ("Gems").

If the philosophy on which the poem operates is slightly foolish, the remainder is altogether delightful. The play on the word *zone* brings in cosmic implications to outdo the geography of the preceding elegy (though geographical analogy is also used here). "That harmonious chyme" has intriguing overtones; it is not the chiming of a timepiece, but rather that of the lady's garments as they are being removed. The sound unmistakably means "bed time." (The lady's compliance is itself a type of harmonious chime announcing bedtime.)

Donne gives a new twist to the conventional Petrarchan figure of (say) the envied handkerchief in the lady's bosom. Here "that happy busk" is envied: the corset-stay "still can be, and still can stand so nigh"—it not only has the privilege of close contact, but it can remain motionless at close range, unlike the speaker's flesh, which in similar circumstances would be set upright. (The first *still* may also refer to restraint of enthusiastic praise.) There is—in Freudian terms—displacement from above to below, in the figure of the "wyerie Coronet" and the "haiery Diademe." In the matter of concealing natural beauty, the intricated underpinnings of the lower regions are to the pubic hairs, as a coronet would be to a lady's coiffure.

In the following couplet there are ambiguities centering around *safely* and *tread*: "Now off with those shoes, and then safely tread/In this loves hallow'd temple, this soft bed." The lady may tread safely here without her shoes, because the bed is soft. In another sense, shoes are a hazard to intercourse; without them, one may safely tread (a barnyard term for copulating). In a third sense, the bed has a certain sanctity as "loves hallow'd temple"; the ritual requires removal of one's shoes.

Lines 31 and 32 quibble on legalistic terms. In entering the bonds of physical love (if not of matrimony), the speaker paradoxically becomes free ("Licence my roaving hands," he has begged). "Then where my hand is set, my seal shall be." I pledge to fulfill my debts to the specific place where my hand is set. In turn I am entitled to a seal of exclusive ownership:

PRIVATE PARTS

NO TRESPASSING

Grierson suspects that the correct reading of line 46 is that of the MSS.: "Here is no penance, much less innocence." He still prefers the 1669 reading, however, believing it "a softening of the original to make it compatible with the suggestion that the poem could be read as an epithalamium." I also prefer the latter reading, but for a different reason. The lady is to "cast all, yea, this white lynnen hence,/There is no pennance due to innocence." The pair, that is, are engaging in innocent merriment for which no pennance is due; the lady need hold back no longer. The speaker would inevitably claim that the act was innocuous in "loves hallow'd temple," whether or not it occurred in marriage.

The concluding couplet of the poem is presumably based on the fancy that men, in the strife of existence, need more armor (clothing) than the sheltered ladies. If even the speaker is naked, what excuse has the lady for holding back? To transfer to this context the concluding lines of "The Dampe" (departing from the reading Grierson prefers):

> . . . Doe you but try
> Your passive valor, and you shall finde than,
> Naked you' have odds enough of any man.
> (Ll. 22-24.)

The foe, indeed, "Is tir'd with standing though he never fight."

## 4

An Epithalamion, Or mariage Song on the Lady Elizabeth, and Count Palatine being married on St. Valentines day

### I

Haile Bishop Valentine, whose day this is,
    All the Aire is thy Diocis,

And all the chirping Choristers
And other birds are thy parishioners,
5      Thou marryest every yeare
The Lirique Larke, and the grave whispering Dove,
The Sparrow that neglects his life for love,
The household Bird, with the red stomacher,
     Thou mak'st the black bird speed as soone,
10  As doth the Goldfinch, or the Halcyon;
The husband cocke lookes out, and straight is sped,
And meets his wife, which brings her feather-bed.
This day more cheerfully then ever shine,
This day, which might enflame thy self, Old Valentine.

## II

15  Till now, Thou warmd'st with multiplying loves
     Two larkes, two sparrowes, or two Doves
       All that is nothing unto this,
For thou this day couplest two Phoenixes;
     Thou mak'st a Taper see
20  What the sunne never saw, and what the Arke
(Which was of soules, and beasts, the cage, and park,)
Did not containe, one bed containes, through Thee,
     Two Phoenixes, whose joyned breasts
Are unto one another mutuall nests,
25  Where motion kindles such fires, as shall give
Yong Phoenixes, and yet the old shall live.
Whose love and courage never shall decline,
But make the whole year through, thy day, O Valentine.

## III

Up then faire Phoenix Bride, frustrate the Sunne,
30     Thy selfe from thine affection
      Takest warmth enough, and from thine eye
All lesser birds will take their Jollitie.
      Up, up, faire Bride, and call,
Thy starres, from out their severall boxes, take
35  Thy Rubies, Pearles, and Diamonds forth, and make
Thy selfe a constellation, of them All,

And by their blazing, signifie,
That a Great Princess falls, but doth not die;
Bee thou a new starre, that to us portends
40 Ends of much wonder; And be Thou those ends.
Since thou dost this day in new glory shine,
May all men date Records, from this thy Valentine.

### IIII

Come forth, come forth, and as one glorious flame
    Meeting Another, growes the same,
45     So meet thy Fredericke, and so
To an unseparable union growe.
        Since separation
Falls not on such things as are infinite,
Nor things which are but one, can disunite,
50 You're twice inseparable, great, and one;
    Goe then to where the Bishop staies,
To make you one, his way, which divers waies
Must be effected and; when all is past,
And that you're one, by hearts and hands made fast,
55 You two have one way left, your selves to'entwine,
Besides this Bishops knot, or Bishop Valentine.

### V

But oh, what ailes the Sunne, that here he staies,
    Longer to day, then other daies?
    Staies he new light from these to get?
60 And finding here such store, is loth to set?
        And why doe you two walke,
So slowly pac'd in this procession?
Is all your care but to be look'd upon,
And be to others spectacle, and talke?
65     The feast, with gluttonous delaies,
Is eaten, and too long their meat they praise,
The masquers come too late, and'I thinke, will stay,
Like Fairies, till the Cock crow them away.
Alas, did not Antiquity assigne
70 A night, as well as day, to thee, O Valentine?

### VI

They did, and night is come; and yet wee see
    Formalities retarding thee.
    What meane these Ladies, which (as though
They were to take a clock in peeces,) goe
75     So nicely about the Bride;
A Bride before a good night could be said,
Should vanish from her cloathes, into her bed,
As Soules from bodies steale, and are not spy'd.
    But now she is laid; What though shee bee?
80  Yet there are more delays, For, where is he?
He comes, and passes through Spheare after Spheare,
First her sheetes, then her Armes, then any where.
Let not this day, then but this night be thine,
Thy day was but the eve to this, O Valentine.

### VII

85  Here lyes a shee Sunne, and a hee Moone here,
    She gives the best light to his Spheare,
    Or each is both, and all, and so
They unto one another nothing owe,
    And yet they doe, but are
90  So just and rich in that coyne which they pay,
That neither would, nor needs forbeare, nor stay;
Neither desires to be spar'd, nor to spare,
    They quickly pay their debt, and then
Take no acquittances, but pay again;
95  They pay, they give, they lend, and so let fall
No such occasion to be liberall.
More truth, more courage in these two do shine,
Then all thy turtles have, and sparrows, Valentine.

### VIII

And by this act of these two Phenixes
100   Nature againe restored is,
    For since these two are two no more,
Ther's but one Phenix still, as was before.

# Off With That Girdle!

        Rest now at last, and wee
        As Satyres watch the Sunnes uprise, will stay
105  Waiting, when your eyes opened, let out day,
        Onely desir'd, because your face wee see;
        Others neare you shall whispering speake,
        And wagers lay, at which side day will breake,
        And win by'observing, then, whose hand it is
110  That opens first a curtaine, hers or his;
        This will be tryed to morrow after nine,
        Till which houre, wee thy day enlarge, O Valentine.

Donne is speaking here as a sort of unofficial poet laureate. We have no record of its reception by the royal pair, but the poem's strong physical bias was hardly unprecedented in the epithalamium genre. Donne's work was cut out for him: a romantic wedding of royalty on St. Valentine's Day, with bird symbolism ready-made (since birds supposedly chose mates on this day). Wisely avoiding the pitfalls (or—should we say?—birdlime) of tedious allegory, Donne uses the conventional symbolism for framework—with particular emphasis on his favored image of the phoenix.

The opening stanza adroitly set the tone and the smybolism at once. St. Valentine is the bishop of love (a religion in its own rite), and his parishioners are birds—an abundance of born choristers. Physical love as a theme, is introduced subtly in the traditionally lecherous sparrow who dies for love at his own cost, the blackbird whose speed love increases, the hen who brings her own featherbed along.

It may be pure coincidence, but this poem resembles "The Canonization" in its coupling of the phoenix with the taper. In the latter poem the tapers have a complex function (see Chapter 5, below, for an analysis of "The Canonization") Here, in addition to its obvious function, the taper may (like its counterpart in the other poem) convey the impression of a tapering-off, a flame which is not renewed—as contrasted with the self-renewing flame of the phoenix. St. Valentine makes "a Taper see/What the sunne never saw"; the taper here represents both night (artificial illumination, as opposed to sunlight) and privacy (of the bed-chamber)—and perhaps also a variety of miracle (something new under the sun). (At any rate, the faint light of the taper reveals what the sun's blaze of light cannot.) Until this miracle occurred, the phoenix was the only one of its kind, but here there are two nonpareils. Noah's Ark carried animals in pairs; the phoenix naturally could not have gone aboard as one each—or, at least, the Ark could not have contained two phoenixes.

At this point we might pause sadly to note that when a scholar is subjective, he can go as far wrong as a subjective critic can. Don Cameron Allen, in a commentary on this passage, observes that "If . . . one reads this section in the light of 1640, one gets a very different poetic reaction than the average modern reader is likely to have."[12] Allen summarizes some very interesting material in the theological controversy over whether the phoenix was aboard the Ark, or whether it ever existed at all. "After [a certain] great authority had expressed himself [the phoenix never on the Ark]," says Allen, "no theologian, and certainly not John Donne, felt able to support the discredited patristic position."[13]—This passage proves nothing of the sort (though external evidence may prove the patristic position discredited): it proves merely that Donne took the side of the argument which gave him imaginative support (if he took sides at all; his statement is ambigious). (Regarding imagery drawn from controversial questions, see Chapter 1, above.) There is no reason whatever to believe that the reader of 1640 had "a very different poetic reaction" from that of the modern reader with some knowledge of the phoenix and the Ark.

*Courage,* in line 27, is equivalent to the *corage* of Chaucer's *Merchant's Tale;* it is simply *sexual desire.* If we have any doubts, we may consult lines 97f.: "More truth ,more courage in these two do shine,/Then all thy turtles have, and sparrows, Valentine." They have the truth (fidelity) of turtledoves, and the courage (sexual appetite) of sparrows. Perhaps the noble overtones on *courage,* plus its association here with words like *love* and *truth,* palliate to some extent the implication of lust.

In the middle of the third stanza, the phoenix figure is abandoned temporarily, in favor of an astronomical analogy: the bride's jewels are stars, and in wearing them she makes herself a constellation. " . . . By their blazing [she is to] signifie,/That a Great Princess falls, but doth not die . . ." The reference to blazing, links this with the basic phoenix imagery. In intensity the blazing denotes magnitude ("a Great Princess") and the falling of a star (which in folklore indicates that a soul is en-route to Heaven). Though the bride is falling from the state of virginity, the time is not yet ripe for her to die.—The figure changes slightly, and she is a stationary new star whose appearance is a portent that a great wonder (the bride herself) is in the offing.

The pair are "twice inseparable, great, and one"; i. e., they are doubly inseparable—because they are great ("separation/ Falls not on such things as are infinite"), and because they are figuratively "one glorious flame." There are three ways in which their entwinement may be effected: Bishop Valentine's romantic way, the Anglican bishop's official way, and a third way which is only within the power of the lovers themselves.

As a representative of the lovers, the poet impatiently chafes under the delays to consummation. The moment finally arrives, however, and the seventh stanza returns to close reasoning, after passages of description. The figures become astronomical again—this time in terms of the masculine sun and the feminine, satellite moon. As the stanza begins, however, the familiar symbolism is reversed: "shee Sunne"—"hee Moone." She gives the best light (place of alighting) to the sphere which is his bay window.—The fancy alters, and each is thought of as both (alternately) sun and moon, and hence—by specious reasoning—all (both sun and moon: the entirety of the pair). Since neither is satellite to the other, neither owes the other a marital debt—or rather they *do* owe each other such debts, but each is so magnanimous in payment that there hardly seems to be a question of debt at all.

Through the act of love the two phoenixes become one, and nature's balance is restored. St. Valentine's Day is extended until nine of the next morning, at which time bets will be laid on which of the pair will show first—"at which side day will breake." The phoenix pair have died, but they will rise again.

HIC LICET IN OCCIDVO CINERE ASPICIT EVM
CVJVS NOMEN EST ORIENS.

# 4

## The Poet as Lawyer

In his review of Rugoff's book on the imagery of Donne, George Williamson questions Rugoff's assumptions regarding the legal imagery: ". . . Although Donne was interested in law, legal imagery is not very prominent in his work; hence he must have felt that legal imagery had been overworked. To this inference some readers might oppose the proposition that legal casuistry appears in the dialectical mode of his work."[1] This chapter will be concerned, in a non-technical way, with three poems which utilize the dialectical mode. Of course, we have already encountered Donne's use of argumentation in verse. Here we will observe the operation of the mode in "The Flea," a lucid poem which is typical of Donne's dialectic, and in "The Extasie" and "Satyre II," problem-poems which are not particularly typical of the mode.

In all three poems the speaker is arguing a case; in poems of this type he may or may not resort to casuistry. If he does. we may be called on to decide whether or not the listener is taken in. If the listener is a woman, seduction—or, at least, amorous persuasion—is likely to be involved. After a session with the technical language of Donne's love lyrics, we are amused to find "Satyre II" ridiculing the poet-lawyer's inept attempts at love-making (he wooes in abstruse legal terminology). It is ironic that Dryden has—mistakenly, it would seem—preferred much the same charge against Donne. "He affects the metaphysicks," Dryden complains, "not only in his satires, but in his amorous verses, where Nature only should reign; and perplexes the minds of the fair sex with nice speculations of philosophy, when he should engage their hearts, and entertain them with the softnesses of love."[2]

Metaphysical density, Dryden seems to be saying, is not necessarily out of place in satire, but in love-poetry "Nature only should reign": spontaneity should drive out artificial mannerisms. Philosophical speculations are altogether too deep for the fair sex; only sentimental drivel can "engage their hearts." Dryden is here verging on the sinceritas heresy—or perhaps it is only the affective fallacy. At any rate, Dryden implies that Donne, in wooing actual women, makes the mistake of addressing them in unconvincing intellectualist terms. If (as seems to be the case) Dryden is wrong about the utilitarian motives of the poet, he is still probably right about the inefficiency of the approach. In terms of seduction, we could imagine the argument of "The Flea" as occurring in real life, but the speaker's sophistry could hardly convince any young lady not already willing to be convinced. To paraphrase Ogden Nash's "Reflections in Ice-Breaking":

> Donne
> Is fun
> But liquor
> Is quicker.

## 2

### The Flea

Marke but this flea, and marke in this,
How little that which thou deny'st me is;

It suck'd me first, and now sucks thee,
And in this flea, our two bloods mingled bee;
5 Thou know'st that this cannot be said
A sinne, nor shame, nor losse of maidenhead,
    Yet this enjoyes before it wooe,
      And pamper'd swells with one blood made of two,
    And this ,alas, is more than wee would doe.

10 Oh stay, three lives in one flea spare,
Where wee almost, yea more than maryed are.
This flea is you and I, and this
Our mariage bed, and mariage temple is;
Though parents grudge, and you, w'are met,
15 And cloystered in these living walls of Jet.
    Though use make you apt to kill mee,
    Let not to that, self murder added bee,
    And sacrilege, three sins in killing three.

Cruell and sodaine, hast thou since
20 Purpled thy naile, in blood of innocence?
Wherein could this flea guilty bee,
Except in that drop which it suckt from thee?
Yet thou triumph'st, and saist that thou
Find'st not thy selfe, nor mee the weaker now;
25     'Tis true, then learne how false, feares bee;
    Just so much honor, when thou yeeld'st to mee,
    Will wast, as this flea's death tooke life from thee.

In this poem seduction seems to be a sort of ritual undergone in lieu of the marriage ceremony. We gather that the lady addressed finds (or chooses to find) the concluding argument unanswerable, and surmise that she had no basic objections to begin with. The ritual consists in a mock battle of wits, with the outcome virtually assured; it is the give-and-take which is pleasurable.

The presence of the lady is made manifest vividly, since the speaker must alter his argument to meet her objections. Without a trace of compunction, she destroys Exhibit A—only to find that her opponent's case is stronger without this item of evidence. At first the flea symbolizes the paltriness of the favor she is withholding. It then represents, in its sucking of blood from the two, that mingling of blood which (according to Renaissance medical belief) occurs in intercourse leading to procreation.[3] Bloods were literally mingled in the marriage bed, the Renaissance thought—not merely racial, national, or family strains.

This mingling is perfectly innocuous in the symbol—why not in the persons it represents?—We are not told precisely how the *flea* "enjoyes before it wooe." Presumably the mingling process affords the 'flea pleasure of the type which intercourse would provide it. At any rate, like a pampered expectant mother, it "swells with one blood made of two."

According to Petrarchan convention, ladies were wont to kill their lovers with scorn. Much more is involved here in the destruction of Exhibit A: not only murder, but suicide (the lady herself being present symbolically in the flea) and even sacrilege (destruction of the temple of their love). Despite his entreaty, the blow descends, and the speaker brims over with mock indignation at this slaughter of the innocent. The lady exults in the fact that they have come through unscathed: the symbolism is invalid. Whereupon, reversing the dialectic, the speaker appropriates the lady's conclusions to his own use: they have come through unscathed in this incident—in her yielding, the lady's honor will fare equally well.

3

### The Extasie

Where, like a pillow on a bed,
    A Pregnant bank swel'd up, to rest
The violets reclining head,
    Sat we two, one anothers best.

5    Our hands were firmly cimented
        With a fast balme, which thence did spring,
    Our eye-beams twisted, and did thred
        Our eyes upon one double string;
    So to'entergraft our hands, as yet
10       Was all the meanes to makes us one,
    And pictures in our eyes to get
        Was all our propogation.
    As 'twixt two equall Armies, Fate
        Suspends uncertaine victorie,
15    Our soules, (which to advance their state,
        Were gone out,) hung 'twixt her, and mee.
    And whil'st our soules negotiate there,
        Wee like sepulchrall statues lay;
    All day, the same our postures were,
20       And wee said nothing, all the day.
    If any, so by love refin'd,
        That he soules language understood,
    And by good love were growen all minde,
        Within convenient distance stood,
25    He (though he knew not which soule spake,
        Because both meant, both spake the same)
    Might thence a new concoction take,
        And part farre purer then he came.
    This Extasie doth unperplex
30       (We said) and tell us what we love,
    Wee see by this, it was not sexe,
        Wee see, we saw not what did move:
    But as all severall soules containe
        Mixture of things, they know not what,
35    Love, these mixt soules, doth mixe againe,
        And makes both one, each this and that.
    A single violet transplant,
        The strength, the colour, and the size,
    (All which before was poore, and scant,)
40       Redoubles still, and multiplies.
    When love, with one another so
        Interinanimates two soules,
    That abler soule, which thence doth flow,

Defects of lonelinesse controules.
45   Wee then, who are this new soule, know,
     Of what we are compos'd, and made,
For, th'Atomies of which we grow,
     Are soules, whom no change can invade.
But O alas, so long, so farre
50     Our bodies why doe wee forbeare?
They are ours, though they are not wee, Wee are
     The intelligences, they the spheares.
We owe them thankes, because they thus,
     Did us, to us, at first convey,
55  Yeelded their forces, sense, to us,
     Nor are drosse to us, but allay.
On man heavens influence workes not so,
     But that it first imprints the ayre,
Soe soule into the soule may flow,
60     Though it to body first repaire.
As our blood labours to beget
     Spirits, as like soules as it can,
Because such fingers need to knit
     That subtile knot, that makes us man:
65  So must pure lovers soules descend
     T'affections, and to faculties,
Which sense may reach and apprehend,
     Else a great Prince in prison lies.
To'our bodies turne wee then, that so
70     Weake men on love reveal'd may looke;
Loves mysteries in soules doe growe,
     But yet the body is his booke.
And if some lover, such as wee,
     Have heard this dialogue of one,
75  Let him still marke us, he shall see
     Small change, when we'are to bodies gone.

Pierre Legouis has an analysis of "The Extasie" by which the poem is considered a study in seduction.[4] Several refutations of Legouis have appeared,[5] and it should be fairly evident by now that Legouis's position is untenable: "The Extasie" is not a seduction poem, nor is it in revolt against Renaissance Neo-Platonism (which seldom ignores physical love altogether). Unlike the case of "The Flea," there is no barrister here pleading for a surrender of chastity, but the speaker is nonetheless reviewing evidence pro and con—perhaps in the manner of a lawyer in summarizing his case, or of a judge in weighing testimony. The verdict sought is a just statement of what Grierson calls "the interconnexion and mutual dependence of body and soul."

This poem is doubly central in importance: Donne is constantly preoccupied with the body-soul relationship, and this poem is so conservative in its conclusions that even Dr. Donne the priest would probably have found its thesis unexceptionable. I am admittedly on dangerous ground here, since most critics find Jack Donne's argument for physical love, in this poem—and Dr. Donne's argument against physical love, in the Sermons—somewhat more vehement than I am willing to concede. Donne's later views on sex, at any rate, will be discussed in Chapter 6, below.

"The Extasie" begins with exposition—the speaker evidently recounting to his beloved, what has just passed between them. Awkward as it is, the device is probably necessary, since the communication peculiar to ecstasy is of the non-verbal sort. We would have had to understand "soules language" to grasp what was going on, as it happened before our sharpened perceptions.

The statement of the poem (if we may summarize it tentatively here) is that—in human relationships—bodies are necessary mediums to the communication of souls. That is the explicit statement, but the statement implicit in the situation, is that ecstasy—a temporary abandonment of body by soul—is a very rare state, a spot-of-time or epiphany remote from everyday experience. If we seek, then, a more accessible means of communication on the level of souls, we must resort to the aid which bodies can give.

In a sense, of course, the ecstasy is made possible by the bodies' co-operation, since the souls evidently emanate from the eyes: "Donne's *Ecstasy* follows the pattern of love in Castiglione's *The Courtier,* for the spirits going from the eyes are identified with the soul which they closely resemble, and by means of the spirits the soul is freed from its prison. . . ."[6] Miss Finney, from whom the quotation is taken, proceeds to cite lines 7f., 15f., and 59-68 ,thereby implying that the "great Prince" of the third passage is freed by ecstasy, rather than—as the context indicates—by an effect more accessible to lovers. There is nothing is the poem saying that "by means of the spirits the soul is freed from its prison."

The word *Pregnant* ingeniously sets up the paradox of lines 10f., with its pun on begetting: "pictures in our eyes to get/ Was all our propagation." "As yet," that is; the latter part of the poem discusses other "meanes to make us one." For the time being, however, the souls commune, and discover for the first time that the ultimate end of their love is such communion —not "sexe," which (as we are told later) is merely an instrument. (Donne's use of *sex* is very close to the modern meaning.)

There are apparently-conflicting statements made regarding the unity of souls. An analogy is based on the fact that "all severall soules containe/Mixture of things, they know not what." Later however, the speaker comments that "Wee . . . know,/Of what we are compos'd, and made/For, th'Atomies of which we grow,/Are soules, whom no chance can invade." There can be no doubt, I think, that for Donne the soul—as opposed to the body—is simple in its immortality. "What ever dyes," we are told in "The good-morrow," was not mixt equal-

ly." The local difficulty in "The Extasie" apparently arises from
a deliberate shift in the meaning of *soules*. *All severall soules*
thus seems to equate *all individual persons,* while the *soules* of
the second reference are entities purely spiritual in nature.

Mortal beings are "not mixt equally": they are made up of
conflicting elements. "Love, these mixt soules [individual per-
sons], doth mixe againe,/And makes both one, each this and
that." *One* here has several layers of meaning. The two souls
(individuals) are reduced to a single soul (spiritual entity)—
with what was formerly *each,* identical with what was formerly
*other.* Love can effect this mixture only by first making "both
one"—by reducing each of the souls (persons) to a soul
(spiritual entity). "When love, with one another so/Interinani-
mates two soules [individuals],/That abler soul [spiritual en-
tity], which thence doth flow,/Defects of lonelinesse controules
[overrides the handicap of mixed nature in the individual per-
son]." The lovers, then, know what they ("this new soule") are
made of: each component is a changeless soul, and hence "no
change can invade" the compound, "mixt equally" as it is.

The emphasis here has been placed rather heavily on spiritual entities. Consequently, the speaker hastens to give the body
its due: "But O alas, so long, so farre/Our bodies why doe wee
forebare?" There was no need for bodies during the ecstasy, but
the body's services must not be slighted merely because they are
everyday—rather than rare—in occurrence. The bodies are owed
"thankes, because they thus,/Did us, to us, at first convay. . . ."
Sex, as they discovered, was not the ultimate end, but it proved
an effective means.

The bodies "Yeelded their forces, sense, to us,/Nor are
drosse to us, but allay." Empson has a valuable commentary on
this passage:

. . . The antithesis for *allay* makes it mean 'alloy,' a less valuable substance put into their gold to strengthen it for practical use; *allay* could mean 'keeping the spiritual pleasure from being too great, more than our strength could bear,' which goes with 'alloy,' then, behind that, 'relief to the pain of desire,' which makes the flesh less unimportant. This is reinforced by the special meaning of sense ('the wanton stings and motions of the s'). That rich word confuses the pleasure and the knowledge given by the senses (Donne wants to imply they are mutually dependent) and suggests that soul and body are in a healthy intuitive relation—'plenty of sense.' The use of *sense* for sensibleness became stronger later in the century, but it is already clearly an element in the word—for example in saying 'there is no sense' in a statement when it has meaning but is not sensible. 'We could not know each other at all without sensations, therefore cannot know each other fully without sensuality, nor would it be sensible to try to do so.'[7]

I am not sure that all these implications are in the passage. In his later work Empson makes out a stronger case for *sense* as a key word in Shakespeare and in Wordsworth, where certain effects are gained by reiteration in long poems.[8] At any rate, *allay* has a key function in this poem, by virtue of its layers of meaning. The primary implication is, I think, one suggested—but not dwelled on—by Empson. As Rugoff notes, Donne is exceptionally fond of coin imagery. Here the lovers' spiritual relationship is figuratively a coin of pure gold. For the practical purposes of everyday life, however, the gold must be mixed with a stronger—if less valuable—metal. The alloy is baser, but not base. (The phrasing does not demand that a coin—rather than plate, for example—be referred to in connection with the alloy. But Donne's fondness for coin imagery can hardly be exaggerated, and we shall see later that Donne has used one type of such imagery to represent an adaptation of spiritual values to ordinary human comprehension.)

Grierson has, I think, led his successors astray by reading

"heavens influence" as that of the heavenly bodies. The reference seems to be, rather, to a bit of Scholastic lore featured in "Aire and Angels." In their ministrations to human beings, angels take on bodies of air. (Compare the following from the Sermons: "From extreme to extreme, from east to west, the angels themselves cannot come, but by passing the middle way between. . . ."[9] Churches, that is, are not to be judged in terms of black-or-white; even the Roman Church—Donne might say— has good as well as bad qualities.) To return to "The Extasie,"

> On man heavens influence workes not so,
> But that it first imprints the ayre,
> Soe soule into the soule may flow,
> Though it to body first repaire.
> (Ll. 57-60.)

The *so* of line 57 does not refer to a previous description, as one commentator has apparently assumed.[10] The statement of lines 57f. is simply that angels must assume bodies of air before they minister to human beings. A similar use of *so* and *but that* occurs in the Sermons: ". . . In this sea [of existence], God holds no man up by the chin so, but that if he sin in confidence of that sustentation, he shall sink."[11] In the rare state of ecstacy, soul flows into soul as a matter of course. If angels utilize bodies in ministering to human souls, however, so—on an everyday basis—may human souls commune through the agency of bodies. (*Though it to body first repaire* may refer, in a secondary sense, to sex and its groping towards spiritual communion.)

According to the old physiology, the spirits of the blood acted as intermediaries between body and soul. If lovers' souls ignore the body's existence, they are courting spiritual isolation, with all the consequent "Defects of lonelinesse." To this consideration is added the fancy—a recurrent one in the love poems —that the present lovers are far above the laity in their ability to transcend physical love. They must not, by disdaining the flesh, set up stumbling blocks for weaker human beings. The body, after all, is love's usual mode of communication.

The last four lines of the poem raise certain difficulties. We are puzzled about the tone of *Small change*. This phrase may mean that the lovers will be content with holding hands and gazing at each other soulfully (what they have just been doing). We would gather, however, that the lovers have something more intimate in mind. An objection arises immediately: *Small change* would, improbably, bear heavy ironic connotations.— The usual critical comment is that the relationship will be just as pure afterwards as it was before—a very inept way of evading the issue.

*This dialogue of one* harks back to the first mention of the onlooker, who would not know "which soule spake,/Because both meant, both spake the same." In one sense, the whole poem is a "dialogue of one": it is a monologue representing the opinions of both lovers. And it is certainly absorbed in the dialectics of unity. We might say that the unity of bodies is to rival the unity of souls, but in visual terms the implications are still disconcerting.—It seems to me that the final lines echo (with a difference) the coin imagery of line 56. A coin of pure gold— we have postulated—symbolizes the lovers' communion of souls in ecstasy. Let the onlooker mark this coin. *Still marke us* means *continue to observe us,* but also *mark us [the coin] while we remain immobile.* Before the onlooker's eyes, the coin will become small change. The naked spirit is beyond the grasp of normal human comprehension. "Sense," however, may serve as alloy, to adapt the goldpiece to practical use. Or "sense" may represent the coins into which the spirit's goldpiece is changed. The exchange rates somehow occasion a certain loss. (One passage in the Sermons [Alford, III, 42] deals with spiritual comprehension in terms of a great piece of coin and lesser pieces;

the latter coins represent an adaptation to ordinary human capacity.)

If my interpretation is correct, the concluding lines are based on somewhat private symbolism, by which *small change* virtually equates *alloy,* as opposed to *dross* (i. e., inferior, but not worthless, metal). In verse and prose, Donne refers to the polytheistic watering-down of God, in terms of changing a single valuable coin into coins of lesser worth. Here are the pertinent lines in *Of the Progresse of the Soule*:

> . . . The Heathen made them severall gods,
> Of all Gods Benefits, and all his Rods,
>
> * * *
>
> And . . . by changing that whole precious Gold
> To such small Copper coynes, they lost the old,
> And lost their only God, who ever must
> Be sought alone, and not in such a thrust. . . .
> (Ll. 425-432.)

The prose statement runs remarkably close: "Money that is changed into small pieces is easily lost; . . . we know the heathens lost the true God, in a thrust [jostling crowd]; they made so many false gods, of every particular quality, and attribute of God, that they scattered him, and evacuated him, to an utter vanishing. . . ."[12] If the reader is still skeptical about my interpretation here, I can only refer him to the text and let him profit *en bloc* from the richness of implication. In the words of Donne, regarding a sermon text, " . . . This day we shall . . . not so much distribute the text into an explication of the particular words (which is, as the mintage and coining of gold into several lesser pieces) as to lay up the whole wedge, and ingot of gold all at once in you. . . ."[13]

I should make clear beyond question, the grounds on which I claim for *Small change* a meaning close to the modern mean-

ing of the phrase. There is a temptation to invoke the doctrine
that a poem may grow and hence take on meanings which—according
to historical evidence—were not available to the poet
who wrote it.[14] Whatever the merits of this doctrine, I prefer
not to invoke it here. It is altogether unlikely that *Small change*
could have had for Donne's time its precise modern implication
as a common phrase. But here, as in the case of *Spittles of
diseases* (see Chapter 1, above), the modern implications—I
think—give us by accident a key to the contemporary tone of
the phrase. In this particular case, Donne's phrase seems to be
highly condensed—*Small change* representing "money that is
changed into small pieces. . . ." This condensation is necessary,
for the sake of the ambiguity: 1. Small change will ensue (i. e.,
no change at all—this being conventional understatement); 2.
Actual change will ensue—though it be quantitatively small.

*Small change*, with or without my reading, may conceal a
minor paradox. The change will be small, but the loss will be
inevitable (though not necessarily total). The flesh is given its
due, but no more than its due. As we shall see later, Dr. Donne
the priest—though his imagery in verse and prose retains a firm
grasp on the physical—takes the view that sex in marriage is not
"drosse to us, but allay." It is better to marry than to burn, as
St. Paul put the matter. "The Extasie," though its attitude
towards sex is perhaps not so stark, is far from being a triumphant
affirmation of the flesh. It is, after all, the soul which
is the "great Prince," and not the body—though the body has
potentialities for rescuing the prince from the prison which the
body itself constitutes.

4

## Satyre II

Sir; though (I thanke God for it) I do hate
Perfectly all this towne, yet there's one state

# The Poet as Lawyer

In all ill things so excellently best,
That hate, toward them, breeds pitty towards the rest.
5    Though Poetry indeed be such a sinne
As I thinke that brings dearths, and Spaniards in,
Though like the Pestilence and old fashion'd love,
Ridlingly it catch men; and doth remove
Never, till it be sterv'd out; yet their state
10   Is poore, disarm'd, like Papists, not worth hate.
One, (like a wretch, which at Barre judg'd as dead,
Yet prompts him which stands next, and cannot reade,
And saves his life) gives ideot actors meanes
(Starving himselfe) to live by his labor'd sceanes;
15   As in some Organ, Puppits dance above
And bellows pant below, which them do move.
One would move Love by rithmes; but withcrafts charms
Brings not now their old feares, nor their old harmes:
Rammes, and slings now are seely battery,
20   Pistolets are the best Artillerie.
And they who write to Lords, rewards to get,
Are they not like singers at doores for meat?
And they who write, because all write, have still
That excuse for writing, and for writing ill;
25   But hee is worst, who (beggarly) doth chaw
Other wits fruits, and in his ravenous maw
Rankly digested, doth those things out-spue,
As his owne things; and they are his owne, 'tis true,
For if one eate my meate, though it be knowne
30   The meate was mine, th'excrement is his owne:
But these do mee no harme, nor they which use
To out-swive dildoes, and out-usure Jewes;
To out-drinke the sea, to out-sweare the Letanie;
Who with sinnes all kinds as familiar bee
35   As Confessors; and for whose sinfull sake,
Schoolemen new tenements in hell must make:
Whose strange sinnes, Canonists could hardly tell
In which Commandements large receit they dwell.
But these punish themselves; the insolence
40   Of Coscus onely breeds my just offence,
Whom time (which rots all, and makes botches poxe,
And plodding on, must make a calfe an oxe)

Hath made a Lawyer, which was (alas) of late
But a scarce Poet; jollier of this state,
45  Than new benific'd ministers, he throwes
Like nets, or lime-twigs, wheresoever he goes,
His title of Barrister, on every wench,
And wooes in language of the Pleas, and Bench:
A motion, Lady; Speake Coscus: I have beene
50  In love, ever since *tricesimo* of the Queene,
Continuall claimes I have made, injunctions got
To stay my rivals suit, that hee should not
 Proceed; spare mee; In Hillary terme I went,
You said, If I return'd next size in Lent,
55  I should be in remitter of your grace;
In th'interim my letters should take place
Of affidavits: words, words, which would teare
The tender labyrinth of a soft maids eare,
More, more, then ten Sclavonians scolding, more
60  Then when winds in our ruin'd Abbeyes rore.
When sicke with Poetrie, and possest with muse
Thou wast, and mad, I hop'd; but men which chuse
Law practice for meere gaine, bold soule, repute
Worse than imbrothel'd strumpets prostitute.
65  Now like an owlelike watchman, hee must walk
His hand still at a bill, now he must talke
Idly, like prisoners, which whole months will sweare
That onely suretiship hath brought them there,
And to every suitor lye in every thing,
70  Like a Kings favourite, yea like a King;
Like a wedge in a blocke, wring to the barre,
Bearing like Asses, and more shameless farre
Then carted whores, lye, to the grave Judge; for
Bastardy abounds not in Kings titles, nor
75  Symonie and Sodomy in Churchmens lives,
As these things do in him; by these he thrives.
Shortly (as the sea) hee will compasse all our land;
 From Scots, to Wight; from Mount, to Dover strand.
And spying heires melting with luxurie,
80  Satan will not joy at their sinnes, as hee.
For as a thrifty wench scrapes kitching-stuffe,

And barreling the droppings, and the snuffe,
Of wasting candles, which in thirty yeare
(Relique-like kept) perchance buyes wedding geare;
85  Peecemeale he gets lands, and spends as much time
Wringing each Acre, as men pulling prime.
In parchments then, large as his fields, hee drawes
Assurances, bigge, as gloss'd civill lawes,
So huge, that men (in our times forwardnesse)
90  Are Fathers of the Church for writing lesse.
These hee writes not; nor for these written payes,
Therefore spares no length; as in those first dayes
When Luther was profest, He did desire
Short *Pater nosters,* saying as a Fryer
95  Each day his beads, but having left those lawes,
Addes to Christs prayer, the Power and glory clause.
But when he sells or changes land, he'impaires
His writings, and (unwatch'd) leaves out, *ses heires,*
As slily as any Commenter goes by
100 Hard words, or sense; or in Divinity
As controverters, in vouch'd Texts, leave out
Shrewd words, which might against them cleare the doubt.
Where are those spred woods which cloth'd hertofore
Those bought lands? not built, nor burnt within dore.
105 Wheres th'old landlords troops, and almes? In great hals
Carthusian fasts, and fulsome Bachanalls
Equally I hate; meanes blesse; in rich mens homes
I bid kill some beasts, but no Hecatombs,
None starve, none surfet so; But (Oh) we allow
110 Good workes as good, but out of fashion now,
Like old rich wardrops; but my words none drawes
Within the vast reach of th'huge statute lawes.

So far as chronology is concerned, this satire must have been
written at a time when Donne was at a transitional stage between
the Roman Catholic and the Anglican persuasions. The attitudes
expressed are critical of both faiths, though we are not necessarily justified in the assumption that Donne is here speaking as a
person—for the time, a dissenter against both persuasions. (We

may note that even Dr. Donne was prepared to point out faults and acknowledge virtues where he found them—in Catholicism and Anglicanism alike.) At any rate, the attitudes were quite likely unpopular at the time, and that fact may help to account for the extreme obscurity of the poem: Donne the person would be blamed for the attitudes, by those unsympathetic readers able to understand what he was talking about. When the poem was finally published (in 1633), certain potentially anti-royalist sentiments were excised (moral considerations may have been involved, as well), but the objectionable features would earlier have been (in the main) religious, with political overtones.

The difficulties in this poem spring from inherent obscurity of phrase and passage, as combined with extremely abrupt transitions. Or, rather, of the two major transitions, one is relatively smooth, but the other is almost completely baffling to the reader who fails to realize that the transition is being prepared for, though in unorthodox fashion. The key to both types of obscurity here, lies in the vehicles of metaphors. (The Ricardian tenor-vehicle distinction is being used, and the word *metaphor* represents analogical figures of speech in general. See Chapter 1, above, for an extended discussion of vehicles in Donne.) Here the choice of vehicles is far from arbitrary. In every successful figure (in Donne and elsewhere), the vehicle makes a valuable contribution to the statement of the tenor. In this satire, however, some of the vehicles also tell us what the tenor is about (when we would otherwise be perplexed), or what the general drift of the poem is about.

The poem consists of a monologue addressed to a person who presumably would share the speaker's opinions. Dialogue is extremely rare in Donne's poetry, but it occurs here (ll. 49-57) as reported within the basic monologue—though Coscus's lady is barely able to get a word in edgewise.—Like the Ancient Mariner, the speaker buttonholes a potential listener;

he then proceeds to vent his spleen against his favorite detestations. Poets are not worth hatred—which is to say that they are beneath contempt. At any rate, the speaker describes in some detail—with considerable expenditure of hatred—members of the class of poets (who theoretically aren't worth considering at all). Other detestable creatures are described in briefer detail. The major object of hatred, however, is Coscus—the lawyer and former poet.

Why are the two vocations combined in Coscus? Grierson would evidently reply that Donne is satirizing a contemporary poet's use of legal terminology. There are obvious objections to Grierson's assumption. One objection is that Donne himself (as we have noted) uses technical language in his poetry—and some, though not much, of the terminology is legal. The major point against Grierson, however, is that it is as a person—not as a poet—that Coscus uses such absurd diction. His wooing is carried on in prose, rather than in verse. (The lines carrying the speech are in verse, of course, but we assume by convention that they are delivered in prose.) Coscus's jargon is laughable because it is exceedingly unconvincing in the way of amorous persuasion, and because it demonstrates his pompous infatuation with the title of barrister.

To hark back to Dryden on amorous persuasion, we might say that Donne had no delusions about seduction by gobbledygook. (His assumption to the contrary is a sort of dramatic convention in "The Flea.") "Satyre II" seems to make a pertinent comment on seduction in the description of one type of poetaster:

One would bring Love by rithmes; but witchcraft charms
 Brings not now their old feares, nor their old harmes:
Rammes, and slings now are seely battery,
Pistolets are the best Artillerie.

(Ll. 17-20.)

But it is poetic incantation—not dialectic—which is here labeled inadequate for amorous persuasion. Lines 19f. constitute a sort of vehicle to the tenor in lines 17f.: magical charms have grown outmoded, just as military weapons become obsolete. By means of its pun on *Pistolets,* the vehicle sets the theme of the satire: in these corrupt days, money is the best artillery for political aggrandizement, seduction, what have you. (The diminutive *Pistolets* is not only necessary for the pun on *coins*: it points up the argument from size. Why bother with cumbersome battering rams [love poems], when handy little pistols [coins] can turn the trick?)

We still haven't answered our question about the poet-lawyer combination in Coscus.—The two are combined, I think, mainly for the sake of continuity in the poem. (I am not sure how poetasters and lawyers got to be objects of satire in the same poem, except that in Donne's time many young gentlemen ostensibly studying law, must have been primarily interested in letters.) The neck-verse vehicle (ll. 11-13), at any rate, anticipates the change in subject matter, just as the reference to Papists (l. 10) begins the long series of vehicles which prepare for a more abrupt transition—that from unprincipled greed in Coscus, to the suppression of monasteries in England.

The key vehicles in this transitions, I suppose, are the references to "our ruin'd Abbeyes" and to "men pulling prime." (Other—and cumulative—allusions to religious matters, reflect on Catholic as well as Protestant practices.) Grasping Coscus "spends as much time/Wringing each Acre, as men pulling prime." The implicit contrast is one between personified greed *wringing* land away from others, and personified devotion *ringing* churchbells for a canonical hour. An abbey, prior to ruin, would seem to be the scene of the bell-ringing.

The difficult transition begins with line 103. *Spred* has a double meaning: the woods were formerly *widespread,* but now that the monastic holdings are bought and sold commercially, the timber is distributed like the rest of the Catholic wealth—*spread to the four winds.* No longer serving a constructive purpose, the woods are "not built [to shelter the sick and the poor], nor burnt within dore" as firewood for the needy. The troops of monks have gone, and with them their charitable works. (It is historically true that the poor suffered directly, when the organized charities of the monastic system were cut off.)—The speaker, however, is not advocating a return to the past, but rather a middle-of-the-road policy between past (Carthusian) and present (bacchanalian) excesses. (The Carthusians were noted for the severity of their order; incidentally, they put up one of the most courageous of the losing fights against Henry VIII.) " . . . Meanes blesse. . . ."—riches may be a blessing, if one adheres to the Golden Mean, killing "some beasts, but no Hecatombs" (huge quantities).—A sort of socialism is advocated, but it will never catch on: good works are given lip-service only. The speaker's argument will attract no one who remains "Within the vast reach of th'huge statute lawes"—laws which decreed dissolution of the monasteries, and which now encourage the grasping of which Coscus is the type. *Good workes* has a double implication: 1. behavior as proof of Chrisian persuasion (cf. the faith-works controversy along Protestant-Catholic lines)—greed would hence be outlawed; 2. charitable projects—alms of the type the old system provided.—Without committing himself to Roman Catholicism, the speaker takes a stand against the materialism which the new order has brought.

If the cumulative effect of vehicles is necessary to tell us that the poem closes on a theme of politico-religious controversy, the vehicle is no less essential to interpretation of a passage in the satire which has been repeatedly (and unconvincingly) explicated by commentators. The passage extends from line 65 through line 76, and is considered a standard crux in Donne, though nobody (including me) has a particularly high opinion of the poem in which it is contained. Obviously, Coscus is being described here as a thoroughly despicable member of his profession, but the specific phrasing puzzles us. After Coscus's activities have been described, we are told that "Bastardy abounds not in Kings titles, nor/Symonie and Sodomy in Churchmens lives,/As these things do in him; by these he thrives." *These things* evidently refers to the activities of Coscus, described some lines above, and the vehicle of the figure seems merely to cite classic superlatives of wickedness in other fields. If we look closer, however, we will see that Coscus also thrives by bastardy, simony, and sodomy. The whole passage is so dense in implication that we would do well to paraphrase in detail.

Like a prowling night watchman, Coscus walks with "His hand still at a bill. . . ." The watchman, of course, keeps his "billy" constantly at hand. Coscus, in a slightly different sense, is constantly on the lookout for someone to club—the *bill* in this case being a promissory note which has fallen due, or a blank statement of charges to be filled out when a lawsuit is in the offing. (In modern terms, Coscus is at least as low as an ambulance-chaser.—Perhaps he will threaten legal action if the promissory note is not redeemed.) Like prisoners, Coscus talks idly. Wishing to salve their pride, the prisoners will swear for months on end (*Idly*: 1. to no avail; 2. to pass the time way) that they are in the debtors' prison merely because they generously if ill-advisedly underwrote somebody else's credit rating. Coscus will swear that only concern for his potential client's welfare has brought him to offer his services.

The erotic implications enter at this point. Coscus will lie "to every suitor . . . in every thing/Like a Kings favourite, yea like a King. . . ." The mendacity of Coscus is beyond question, but here the reference is to a different kind of lying: he will lie in every sort of erotic receptacle, at every request—to settle a case out of court, on behalf of his client; or to buy off a judge (an anticipation of the following lines); or merely to hold a client whose business is coveted. With reference to this last sense, a quotation from the Sermons might be pertinent. Certain sins are traditionally associated with certain professions; "Is there. . . . No being a lawyer, without serving the passion of the client?"[15] *Passion* is probably erotic in meaning here; the reference, however, may merely be to pandering, on the basis of wide acquaintance with the underworld—but a type of male prostitution may be involved.

A king's favorite may sell his influence with the king, at the price of a woman's chastity—or the king may dispense with the middleman and enjoy the reward himself. Bastardy, at any rate, abounds in titles to royal authority. *Bastardy* may mean *fornication,* in general, as well as *procreation of bastards,* in particular; bastards get into the royal succession through the lasciviousness of kings, and/or their desire for a male heir. (There may be a side glance here at Henry VIII.)

Lines 71-73 have caused greatest puzzlement to critics. The subject matter is simply that of "Symonie and Sodomy"—simony, that is, accomplished with the aid of sodomy. The term *simony* could apparently equate *bribery* in general, without necessary reference to ecclesiastical matters. See, at least, the *NED*'s 1656 quotation: "Earl Monm. tr. *Boccalini's Advts. fr. Parnass.* I. lxxvii. 103. The prevarication of Advocates, the Symony used of Judges." At any rate, the verb *lye* in line 73 apparently refers to both prevarication (on the obvious level) and simony (sodomy used as a bribe).—But here is a paraphrase of lines 71-73: Like a wedge in a vise, Coscus will twiste (writhe) through the agency of the bar (in one sense, *barre* equates *lever;* in another, *barre* is metonymic for *judge*[*s*]; cf. the use of *bench* in this connection); bearing up similar arses to those borne up by—but, in so doing, considerably more shameless than—whores publicly displayed in a cart for their heterosexual deeds, he will lie at the behest of well-fed, heavy judges (hence the "wringing"). Coscus will get his fee from his client, and the client will get his favorable judgment.

The whores are shameless because they perform actions which invite public censure, but also because—far from being abashed and repentant—they consider their cart-ride as so much free publicity.—The *asses-arses* pun, I think, requires little phonetic documentation. Spellings are helpful here. The dropping of *r* from words whose accented vowel is historically identical with that of *arses,* and the appearance of excrescent *r* in words where it has no historical justification, both point to non-pronunciation of the *r* in Donne's time. *Arse* might then have been pronounced, not only [a:s], but also [æ:s]—phonetically identical with the pronunciation of *ass* at that time.[16]

We may well ask what meaning lines 71-73 could have on the "obvious" level (before being translated into obscene puns). It seems to me quite likely that Grierson's interpretation may be applicable on this level—or Williamson's,[17] if *Bearing-like* (the combination, without Grierson's orthographical hyphen) is too extreme a locution even for a secondary meaning in Donne. (There may be some sort of transitional link between carted whores and asses of the type which would pull their cart.) At any rate, the primary meaning involves so much delving into such a mediocre poem, that it is hardly worth the effort.

# *In Sonnets Pretty Romes*

I HAVE NOT (as the reader may have imagined) discovered a
new variant reading to line 32 of "The Canonization." The title
of this chapter is based on a phonetic pun which may or may
not occur in the line concerned. (It is possible beyond question,
on phonetic grounds; see the analysis of "The Canonization"
in a later section of this chapter.) The important point here is
that such an ambiguity would summarize beautifully Donne's
characteristic combination of sacred and secular love: We'll
build in sonnets pretty [ru:mz].

Corresponding to the necessity for some sort of current belief in the Ptolemaic system, etc. (see Chapter 1, above), there
was the necessity—in Donne's time—for some sort of cross-ten-
sion in figures uniting different spheres of discourse. But
Donne's combination of secular with sacred love, is inadequate
proof of either revolt against Petrarchanism, or ideal masochism
on Donne's part, or even heavy paradox. Petrarchan or Platonic
poetry, though not primarily physical in its approach to love,
sometimes dealt with secular love in terms of sacred love. Rugoff
reminds us that a tendency such as Donne's to couple the two,
"is not unique among Elizabethan poets" (pp. 222 f.). Rugoff
footnotes the statement: "It has, in fact, been connected with the

Platonic but distinctly sensuous tradition of the religion of beauty in woman which flourished in Renaissance Italy. See Jefferson Butler Fletcher's *The Religion of Beauty in Woman,* N. Y., Macmillan, 1911."

Attention will be devoted later to Donne and the problem of sex. With reference to religion and masochism (the latter as a product of blasphemy), we might note here that Donne repented of his earlier undue emphasis on sensuality, not of his coupling of secular with sacred love (which occurs, as we have mentioned, even in the Divine Poems). It is interesting, also, to note that Dr. Johnson, though he had no sympathy for Donne's coupling of the two types of love, was still careful not to accuse Donne of blasphemy. The difference in taste is attributed to the age in which Donne lived. From Donne, Cowley "may have learned that familiarity with religious images, and that light allusion to sacred things, by which readers far short of sanctity are frequently offended; and which would not be borne in the present age, when devotion, perhaps not more fervent, is more delicate."[1]

Donne's use of Roman Catholic sacred imagery is probably no indication of disrespect following upon revulsion. Donne had a prior acquaintance with Roman imagery, and would not choose to neglect its rich imaginative potentialities (from the biographical standpoint, in the Church of England Donne was always more Anglo-Catholic than Protestant).—To resume the matter of secular in combination with sacred love, this particular coupling was not foreign to religious tradition. Witness the allegorical interpretation of The Song of Solomon (if it had not been considered allegorical, it would scarcely have been admitted to the Biblical canon). This Old Testament book traditionally prefigures a spiritual relationship between Christ and his Church, though it deals on the obvious level with the sensuous and the thinly veiled sensual. If we would like the last word on this matter from Donne himself, he is able to supply it. This is Dr. Donne speaking:

> . . . A voluptuous man [in Donne's usage, an epicure], who is turned to God [will] find plenty and deliciousness enough in him, to feed his soul, as with marrow, and with fatness, as *David* expresses it. . . . *Solomon,* whose disposition was amorous, and excessive in the love of women, when he turn'd to God, he departed not utterly from his old phrase and language, but having put a new, and a spiritual tincture, and form and habit in all his thoughts, and words, he conveys all his loving approaches and applications to God, and all Gods gracious answers to his amorous soul, into songs, and Epithalamians, and marriages between God and his Church, and between God and his soul; as we see so evidently in all his other writings, and particularly in this text, *I love them,*&c.[2]

Donne the voluptuous hedonist grew up to be Donne the voluptuous saint.

2

### Aire and Angels

Twice or thrice had I loved thee,
Before I knew thy face or name;
So in a voice, so in a shapeless flame,
*Angells* affect us oft, and worship'd bee;
5     Still when, to where thou wert, I came,
Some lovely glorious nothing I did see.
    But since my soule, whose child love is,
Takes limmes of flesh, and else could nothing doe,
    More subtile than the parent is,
10   Love must not be, but take a body too,
    And therefore what thou wert, and who,
      I bid Love aske, and now
That it assume thy body, I allow
And fixe it selfe in thy lip, eye, and brow.

15 Whilst thus to ballast love, I thought,
   And so more steddily to have gone,
   With wares which would sinke admiration,
   I saw, I had loves pinnace overfraught,

   Ev'ry thy haire for love to worke upon
20 Is much too much, some fitter must be sought;
   For, nor in nothing, nor in things
   Extreme, and scatt'ring bright, can love inhere;
   Then as an Angell, face, and wings
   Of aire, not pure as it, yet pure doth weare,
25   So thy love may be my loves spheare;
   Just such disparitie
   As is twixt Aire and Angells puritie,
   'Twixt womens love, and mens will ever bee.

This is not, strictly speaking, a secular-sacred love poem. It is merely a secular-love poem which utilizes some of the machinery of Scholastic theology. As such, however, it may serve as an introduction to the true mixture of secular and sacred.—"Aire and Angels" is commonly interpreted as reversing its tone and ending in more-or-less gentle cynicism (see, however, George Williamson's analysis, for one dissenting opinion[3]). The poem is undoubtedly complex in structure, but it is none the less unified in tone (I think), for all its intricacies and involvements.

There is a modern popular song called "I Wish I Knew the Name of the Girl in My Dreams." Its implications are far more sentimental than Metaphysical, but the title might almost paraphrase the opening lines of Donne's poem. In this case, however, the face—as well as the name—is an unknown quantity. The speaker has had a sort of unlocalized romantic ardor, and the fancy here is that the lady addressed is a concrete projection of this unlocalized emotion.

In the first stanza, then, the basic theme of the poem is

stated: the necessary projection of the impalpable into the palpable. When angels are first brought in as illustrative material, air is not involved. In this case the angels apparently represent the impalpable as manifested in a semi-palpable state. *Affect* in line 4 is an ambiguity. It can merely mean *influence*: angels so influence us that we accord them worship. But it can also mean that angels take on our human characteristics "in a voice . . . in a shapeless flame"—to the extent that we can worship them, if not recognize them distinctly. At any rate, the remainder of the first stanza clearly anticipates the air-angels motif of the second stanza: the speaker's unlocalized worship is forced to concentrate upon a human form, just as his soul was required to take a body. The lady addressed (to recapitulate) is the concrete embodiment required.

The second stanza opens with a summary and advancement, both in nautical terms, of the first stanza's thought-content. The speaker had intended to ballast love's barque (for steadier sailing) with wares which would sink the ship of mere admiration, but he saw that he had overloaded even love's ship. The concrete particulars were just too breathtaking and overwhelming for human love, which can inhere neither in disembodied spirits nor in the detail of dazzling physical beauty. The speaker's love *does* exist, however; and what is the mode of its existence?—In the simplest terms, it exists (inheres) in the less ethereal love which his beloved manifests towards him.

But why —if the beloved is such an ineffable beauty—is her love less ethereal than that of the speaker?—Simply because its object is less ethereal. In lines 25 to 28, *love* has multiple levels of meaning. It may refer to affection projected towards another person (the usual romantic sense of the noun *love*), but it may also mean *beloved*. This ambiguity sets up a paradox in line 25 (each as the other's sphere): Thy beloved (the man, the clod) may be the sphere governed by my beloved (the woman, the supernal beauty); consequently, thy affection (because it *is* founded on something solid and non-ethereal) may be my affection's sphere of operation.—The figure of lines 23-25 involves two concepts drawn from Scholastic science: the belief that angels take on bodies of air in order to establish communication with mortals; and the concept of a celestial sphere governed by an Influence—the Influence being purer (less corporeal) than the sphere, unlike the particular planet or star, which is merely carried around by the sphere. In the case of angels— as in that of Influences—purity refers to the incorporeal; it must refer to ineffable physical charm, in the case of the woman, and to ethereality of object, in the case of the man's affection. Air is pure (incorporeal) in a relative sense: it is a gas, as opposed to a solid. Though the man's person and the woman's love are disparaged, they are—like the air and the sphere—"yet pure" in a sense (i. e., far from contemptible).

The poem's concluding statement is that the disparity which exists between air's relative purity and angels' absolute purity, will always exist between women's love and men's (because of qualitative differences in object). Paradoxically, the disparagement of women is at the expense of men. Humility, not cynicism, is in evidence here: women's romantic love is inferior, but only because its object is inferior. Similar attitudes of humility may be found elsewhere in literature—with ostensible disparagement of another, hiding actual self-disparagement. Here is Emerson, for example:

> ". . . Have I a lover
>  Who is noble and free?—
> I would he were nobler
>  Than to love me. . . .[4]

Disparagement in such instances is paradoxically praise.

In this poem there are no real analogies drawn between

secular and sacred love. Scholastic angelology is not necessarily subscribed to, nor is there a theological value-judgment expressed in the reference to "Angells puritie" (purely spiritual, as opposed to corporeal, nature). The situation is different, howver (with one possible exception), in the other poems to be discussed in this chapter. Tension develops there between the two antithetical but analogous types of love; in no poem of the chapter, however, is there cynicism involved.

3

## The Canonization

For Godsake hold your tongue, and let me love,
    Or chide my palsie, or my gout,
My five gray haires, or ruin'd fortune flout,
    With wealth your state, your minde with **Arts improve**,
5        Take you a course, get you a place,
        Observe his honour, or his grace,
Or the Kings reall, or his stamped face
    Contemplate, what you will, approve,
    So you will let me love.
10  Alas, alas, who's injur'd by my love?
    What merchants ships have my sighs drown'd?
Who saies my teares have overflow'd his ground?
    When did my colds a forward spring remove?
    When did the heats which my veines fill
15      Adde one more to the plaguie Bill?
Soldiers finde warres, and Lawyers finde out still
    Litigious men, which quarrels move,
    Though she and I do love.

Call us what you will, wee are made such by love;
20    Call her one, mee another flye,
We'are Tapers too, and at our own cost die,
    And wee in us finde the'Eagle and the Dove.
    The Phoenix ridle hath more wit
    By us, we two being one, are it.

25  So to one neutrall thing both sexes fit,
        Wee dye and rise the same, and prove
        Mysterious by this love.

    Wee can dye by it, if not live by love,
        And if unfit for tombes and hearse
30  Our legend bee, it will be fit for verse;
        And if no peece of Chronicle wee prove,
            We'll build in sonnets pretty roomes;
            As well a well wrought urne becomes
    The greatest ashes, as halfe-acre tombes,
35      And by these hymnes, all shall approve
            Us *Canoniz'd* for Love:

    And thus invoke us; You whom reverend love
        Made one anothers hermitage;
        You, to whom love was peace, that now is rage;
40  Who did the whole worlds soule contract, and drove
            Into the glasses of your eyes
                (So made such mirrors, and such spies,
    That they did all to you epitomize,)
            Countries, Townes, Courts: Beg from above
45  A pattern of your love!

Mr. Cleanth Brooks has written such an impressive analysis of this poem,[5] that further comment might seem superflous. There may still be room, however, for a different account—a more detailed account than Mr. Brooks's requirements would permit at the time.

As the poem begins, the speaker is somewhat annoyed by his companion's disparagement of love as unambitious.—I'm not trying to tell *you* how to run *your* life [the speaker says]; you can be as ambitious as you like, just so you leave me alone. You're wasting your time here: I'm committed to love as surely as I'm committed to palsy, gout, greying temples, and poverty. You might as well get on with your political and materialistic ambitions.

## In Sonnets Pretty Romes

What have I done to hurt *you* [the argument continues]? My love is no more harmful than it is helpful; it won't impede commerce, and it won't stop wars. All it does [we have reached the third stanza] is transform our lives [those of his lady and himself] so that everything for us is in terms of love.—With the third stanza we encounter some very subtle ambiguities. The opening line means, You can't think of a phase of our lives which isn't touched by love—but it also means, Use whatever invective you like, we'll turn it to our own account and be proud of it.

The speaker anticipates (in fancy) one term of invective which might be used: the couple as flies (i. e., 1. nobodies without ambition; 2. common lechers). Developing his reply by the association of ideas, the speaker comments: We're not only taper-flies fatally attracted by the flame, we're tapers as well. It's no skin off your nose: we die at our own cost. [The taper's burning consumes itself and nothing else; the lovers die gradually by intercourse, each instance of which deducts a day from their lives—but nobody else is implicated.] We find in us the eagle and the dove [symbols here of the aggressive and the submissive; perhaps the Eagle and the Dove, like the Ram and the Lamb, point to polar manifestations of God's nature (see the discussion of "Holy Sonnet XIV," below); Edgar H. Duncan has noted that, in alchemical terms, the "eagle" and the "dove" are instrumental in the rise of the "phoenix"[6].—As Mr. Brooks notes, the flaming tapers and the birds merge at this point into the fabulous phoenix, a flaming bird which rises from its own ashes. The enigma of the phoenix makes more sense if the bird is taken as a symbol of unity in love. In a way, the phoenix-before and the phoenix-after constitute two beings in one—and so do lovers. The poem's concluding reference to a Platonic Form, leads us to suspect that the "one neutrall thing [to which] both sexes fit," is the double-being of Plato's *Symposium;* once split into a male and a female component, the being as man and woman seeks reunion in love. (Plato also provided, of course, for double-beings with both components of the same sex.) At any rate, in love the two sexes neutralize one another, just as the phoenix-destroyed and the phoenix reborn constitute a single bird with continuity of life.

The lovers "dye and rise the same, and prove/Mysterious by this love." *Mysterious* has backward and forward implications. In a forward sense, it anticipates the sacred imagery of the concluding stanzas: medieval mystery-plays celebrated Christ's dying and rising the same. In a backward sense, of course, the reference is to the "Phoenix riddle." Erotically speaking, the lovers die and rise from bed the same. It is quite possible to push this statement too far. If we examine the erotic implications minutely, we discover an inconsistency in the stanza: the lovers can't rise the same after intercourse, because they die "at their owne cost"—they'll never be the same again. Such an implication is obviously not intended.

What *is* the nature of the enigma, then? It is simply that the lovers can act out the erotic pun on *die. The same,* we might note, is an elusive phrase; one implication is that the lovers are separate individuals before "dying," but a single personality afterwards. The Christian paradox occurs: death as a pathway to fuller life.

A kind of martyrdom is involved in dying for love. (The speaker, in line 28, is answering an objection or potential objection of his companion: that you can't live on love.) The lovers are renouncing voluntarily what seems all-important to the man of worldly ambition. They are quite willing to forego—in death, as in life—the pomp and circumstance accorded to persons of consequence. *Legend* of line 30 has several layers of meaning. As the lovers' life-story, it is suitable for verse. (If the life-story is considered that of saints—a valid meaning of *legend*—we have an anticipation of the secular-sacred imagery which follows.) As their inscribed epitaph, the legend is too insignificant for tombs. As their eulogy, it is too commonplace for hearses. (The *NED* is helpful here: *hearse* in Donne's time might refer to "A temple-shaped structure of wood used in royal and noble funerals. . . . It was decorated with banners, heraldic devices, and lighted candles; and it was customary for friends to pin short poems or epitaphs upon it.")

The lovers hardly expect a citation in the Church's chronicle of major secular events; they will set up their own archives, instead. If a *Rome-room* pun exists here, there may be further anticipation of the sacred imagery which follows. (Other contexts in Donne may or may not support such a phonetic ambiguity. It definitely occurs in Shakespeare; see, for example, *Julius Caesar*, I, ii, 156.) Sonnets might thus constitute romantically-pretty Romes with the ecclesiastical authority to "canonize" themselves as hymns in the liturgy,[7] and ultimately to canonize the poets in love's own religion. In any event, the sonnets become hymns, and the hymns make—or prove—their writers saints. The ashes of the great are memorialized as well in a handsome urn, as in the pretentious tombs of imperial Rome.

Once the lovers are canonized, they will be subject to invocation by less fortunate lovers.—Perhaps Donne's time was too early for *reverend love* to equate in tone *Rev. Smith* (say). At any rate, love's holy rites have made each of the pair the other's hermitage—a paradox, since the very opposite of asceticism is involved, though each has truly renounced the values of the materialistic world.

Beg from above [the less fortunate lovers will say] a sort of Platonic Form which you have established and which we may use now.—Love's saints serve as intermediaries, of course, between human beings and the higher authority corresponding to God in the Church's ecclesiastical order. The saints cannot answer prayers, but in this case they are to entreat for others the blessing of guidance in love according to the pattern which they themselves have set up. Love for them was peace; for their successors, frenzy and confusion. The difference lies in renunciation of the world's restless ambition. The lovers constitute a little world of their own, with the self-sufficiency which they could never attain through political and materialistic schemes.

Chapter 6, below, will devote attention specifically to the microcosm pattern which—here in the "The Canonization"—is combined with the secular-sacred theme. At this juncture we should try to arrive at the way in which secular and sacred interact in the structure of this poem. We have—to begin with—no basis for the assumption that sacred love is being ridiculed. If we were forced to reduce the poem to a single prose statement, we might arrive at something like the following: Secular love is analogous to sacred love in that each demands renunciation of worldly ambition.—Tradition has already set up for Donne the pattern of general relevance between the two types of love. Here romantic love is not attacking religion; it is attacking their common enemy—the materialistic mind. Though the modern reader might consider the enmity exaggerated, between secular love and secular ambition, yet—in the Petrarchan tradition—love is a full-time job. Sighs and tears are not silly; they are expected as a matter of course, and no one should be surprised that they adversely affect business efficiency. We as modern readers are surprised that—clichés of criticism to the contrary—the tears-sighs attitude can exist amicably beside a down-to-earth approach to sex. Such a combination hardly documents the revolt against Petrarchanism we are told to expect in Donne.

In his analysis of this poem, Mr. Brooks has been misled, I think, by two related assumptions—both somewhat questionable: that Donne is embarrassed about the Petrarchanism which crops out in the tone, and that Donne is somewhat apologetic about the use of fantastic imagery. Here is Mr. Brooks:

> Donne accomplishes the modulation of tone ["from the note of irritation with which the poem opens"] by what may be called an analysis of love-metaphor. Here, as in many of his poems, he shows that he is thoroughly self-conscious about what he is doing. This second stanza, he fills with the conventional figures of the Petrarchan tradition: the wind of lovers' sighs, the flood of lovers' tears, etc.—extravagant figures with which the contemptuous secular friend might be expected to tease the lover. The implication is that the poet himself recognizes the absurdity of the Petrarchan love metaphors. But what of it? The very absurdity of the jargon which lovers are expected to talk makes for his argument: their love, however absurd it may appear to the world, does no harm to the world. The practical friend need have no fears: there will still be wars to fight and law suits to argue.

* * *

> The effect of the poet's implied awareness of the lovers' apparent madness is to cleanse and revivify metaphor; to indicate the sense in which the poet accepts it, and thus to prepare us for accepting seriously the fine and seriously intended metaphors which dominate the last two stanzas of the poem.[8]

In later sections of this chapter, I attempt to point out what I consider the error in the popular assumption that Donne, a highly conscious artist, is also a highly self-conscious one. (Lest I seem to quibble over terminology, let me define my terms. A *conscious* artist is well aware of the devices he uses to achieve his purpose; a *self-conscious* artist is uncomfortably aware of his special status as artist, or—in the light of posterity— of his relative position among fellow artists.) Here I cannot see that Donne "recognizes the absurdity of the Petrarchan love metaphors." That is *our* reaction to Petrarchanism, not *his*. Donne would not be embarrassed by the idea of sighs and tears as appropriate to lovers. The companion is objecting— not to the sentimentality of such behavior—but to its inutility for advancing one's fortunes. The speaker's argument in reply is that if it doesn't help, it also doesn't harm; the lover has a right to live his own life.

As for the supposedly fantastic figures, we have no conclusive evidence here or elsewhere that Donne was ever apologetic (even ironically) about using fantastic figures. To believe otherwise, is to imagine that Donne was anticipating and defending himself against post-Johnsonian criticism. Even today the critic has to remind readers that Donne's imagery is not merely fantastic and hence trivial—but Donne himself was not touchy about the matter.

Donne, in various poems, ridicules the idea of Platonic love, and various attitudes usually identified with Petrarchanism; but it is difficult to prove that Donne ever really satirizes the *language* of Petrarchanism. There are contexts where Donne's realism and his Petrarchanism impinge upon one another, and the second stanza of "The Canonization" offers such a context. In the Weeping valediction, the beloved's sighs at parting cause the speaker great pain, and this he objectifies by the fancy that her sighs will encourage the wind to upset his ship. In "'The Canonization," however, the purpose is different, and the technique is different. The speaker points out the fact that merchants' ships are not upset by lovers' sighs. Here the main implication is that lovers live in a world of their own, influencing the secular world for neither good nor ill—but there *is* a touch of realism by implicit contrast with the usual setting for sighs and tears. An analogue occurs in "Elegie XVI," where the lady's charms are described as irresistible, but they will still be powerless to subdue the elements on the voyage she plans to take.

4

## Holy Sonnets

### XIII

What if this present were the worlds last night?
Marke in my heart, O soule, where thou dost dwell,

The picture of Christ crucified, and tell
Whether that countenance can thee affright,
5   Teares in his eyes quench the amasing light,
Blood fills his frownes, which from his pierc'd head fell.
And can that tongue adjudge thee unto hell,
Which pray'd forgiveness for his foes fierce spight?
No, no; but as in my idolatrie
10   I said to all my profane mistresses,
Beauty, of pitty, foulness onely is
A signe of rigour: so I say to thee,
To wicked spirits are horrid shapes assign'd,
This beauteous forme assumes a pitious minde.

## XIV

Batter my heart, three person'd God; for, you
As yet but knocke, breathe, shine, and seeke to mend;
That I may rise, and stand, o'erthrow mee, 'and bend
Your force, to breake, blowe, burn and make me new.
5   I, like an usurpt towne, to'another due,
Labour to'admit you, but Oh, to no end,
Reason your viceroy in mee, mee should defend,
But is captiv'd, and proves weake or untrue.
Yet dearly'I love you,'and would be loved faine,
10   But am betroth'd unto your enemie:
Divorce mee, 'untie, or breake that knot againe,
Take mee to you, imprison mee, for I
Except you'enthrall mee, never shall be free,
Nor ever chast, except you ravish mee.

## XVII

Since she whom I lov'd hath payd her last debt
To Nature, and to hers, and my good is dead,
And her Soule early into heaven ravished,
Wholly on heavenly things my mind is sett.
5   Here the admyring her my mind did whett
To seeke thee God; so streames do shew their head;
But though I have found thee, and thou my thirst hast fed,
A holy thirsty dropsy melts mee yett.
But why should I begg more Love, when as thou

10    Dost wooe my soule for hers; offring all thine:
And dost not only feare lest I allow
My love to Saints and Angels things divine,
But in thy tender jealosy dost doubt
Least the World, Fleshe, year Devill putt thee out.

## XVIII

Show me deare Christ, thy spouse, so bright and clear.
What! is it She, which on the other shore
Goes richly painted? or which rob'd and tore
Laments and mournes in Germany and here?
5    Sleepes she a thousand, then peepes up one yeare?
Is she selfe truth and errs? now new, now outwore?
Doth she, and did she, and shall she evermore
On one, on seaven, or on no hill appeare?
Dwells she with us, or like adventuring knights
10    First travaile we to seeke and then make Love?
Betray kind husband thy spouse to our sights,
And let myne amourous soule court thy mild Dove,
Who is most trew, and pleasing to thee, then
When she'is embrac'd and open to most men.

In these poems we find implicit references to Christ as a delighted cuckold, and to God as a burly rapist or a jealous lover. (There is also a side reference to sexually-obliging mistresses—and to the sexual debts of marriage.) Stated baldly, comparisons of this type seem highly sacrilegious. Even in context, they may repel the squeamish, but most people who read closely enough to recognize what Donne is talking about, should also be able to see that the implications are under strict control.

Empson has an interesting comment on the thirteenth sonnet:

> ... In one's first reading of the first line, the dramatic idea is of Donne pausing in the very act of sin, stricken and swaddled by a black unexpected terror: suppose the end of the world

came *now*? The preacher proceeds to comfort us after this shock
has secured our attention. But looking back, and taking for
granted the end's general impression of security, the first line
no longer conflicts with it. 'Why, this *may* be the last night, but
God is loving. What if it were?' In the first notion one must
collect one's mind to answer the Lord suddenly, and Donne, in
fact, shuffles up an old sophistry from Plato, belonging to the
lyrical tradition he rather despised, and here even more absurdly
flattering to the person addressed and doubtful as to its general
truth than on the previous occasions he has found it handy. Is
a man in the last stages of torture so beautiful, even if blood
hides his frowns? Never mind about that, he is pleased, we have
carried it off all right; the great thing on these occasions is to
have a ready tongue.[9]

In the second edition of *Ambiguity*, a footnote is appended: "I
leave in my expression of distaste for the poem, but it has little
to do with the ambiguity in question."

Empson's distaste is not stated in terms of sacrilege, but it
*does* involve (I think) a misunderstanding of the way in which
the secular-sacred figure operates. (Grierson's choice of variant
readings in line 14, has helped to throw Empson off the track.)
It is quite true that the vehicle of the figure deals with sophistry
in action. Jack Donne handed on to his mistresses that favorite
concept of Neo-Platonism: that beauty or the contrary is an index to benevolence or the contrary. Presumably, no self-respect-
ing woman would admit that she was ugly; she must consequently be good (good to Donne, that is).—Empson apparently
assumes that the deity is being handed the same line of flattery.
(The "person addressed" is actually the poet's soul.) My own
contention is that paradox—not sophistry alone—is in question.
In the secular-sacred figure we have a semi-neutral vehicle. *Pity*
in both cases refers to a granting of the heart's desires; the
object of desire depends on whether "idolatrie" or worship is in
question.

The poem turns on the implications of *affright*: Can Christ's countenance frighten the (presumably contrite) human soul?— The fright may spring either from the hideous appearance of Christ-crucified, or from the fear of damnation. But Christ took on this hideous appearance (and its more significant concomitants) for the sake of the human soul. "This beauteous forme assumes [presupposes] a pitious minde." Here is the paradox: Christ's countenance, *because* it is esthetically hideous, could never frighten a contrite soul. The paradox is stated in terms of a pretense that the ethical beuaty not only *outweighs* the esthetic ugliness—it also transforms it into esthetic beauty.

The tears in Christ's eyes "quench the amasing light," by a sort of filtering process. Again, blood from Christ's head-wounds, fills and obliterates the harsh lines of his frowns. The result is a sort of relative beauty along esthetic lines.—A passage from the Sermons may help us to visualize the situation. Christ-crucified is being described: "There [in the scene evoked] are those *bowells of compassion,* which are so conspicuous, so manifested, as that you may *see them through his wounds.* There those *glorious eyes* grew faint in their light. . . ."[10] The "amasing light" of the poem comes from "those *glorious* [i. e., glory-radiating] *eyes.*" In the first sentence quoted, the phrase *bowells of compassion* operates in a manner analogous to that of *Teares* and *Blood* in the poem. The fact that Christ's bowels were exposed by his voluntarily-accepted wounds, proves conclusively that they were indeed bowels of compassion. (For a fuller discussion of this phrase, see Chapter 2, above.)

In the conluding line of the sonnet, *assumes* is clearly preferable (I think) to the variant reading *assures,* because the former reading supplies all the relevant implications of the latter reading, in addition to implications of its own. The "beauteous forme" assumes the existence of "a pitious minde"—and hence Donne's soul may be reassured. But *assumes* goes beyond *as-*

*sures,* in that it supports more strongly the foregoing argument of the poem. It is not merely the relative beauty which assures the mercy: it is the mercy which causes us to identify ethical with esthetic beauty. There are no extenuating circumstances in the case of wicked spirits; they are ugly by nature, not by self-immolating volition.

Nowhere are we required to accept the Neo-Platonic belief. In the poet's "idolatrie" he had used this concept (whether or not with a straight face) as a sort of seduction propaganda. The implication carries over, from vehicle to tenor, that the concept's value lies wholly in its immediate usefulness. In the tenor the poet is using the concept to express assurance which goes far beyond that which its sophistry (however seriously accepted) could afford.

The critic is justifiably skeptical of effects claimed for metrical stress alone, without reference to the meaning of words in a particular poem or passage. Almost everyone would concede, however, that the stresses in the fourteenth sonnet reinforce the meaning to an unusual degree. The thematic material has to do with battering; and the close juxtaposition of heavily accented syllables connoting violence, conveys a sort of sledgehammer effect. At times the rhythm and alliteration virtually point backward to *Beowulf,* and forward to Hopkins and Auden.

S. L. Bethell makes a perceptive point in connection with this poem and its siege-imagery: " . . . God is the ram (not here the Lamb, we should like to say, but that is a reader's comment, no implication of the poetry)."[11] As a matter of fact, in the seventh of the *La Corona* sonnets, Donne makes this very contrast (and pun) involving the "strong Ramme, which has batter'd heaven for mee," and the "milde Lambe, which with thy blood has mark'd the path. . . ." In the thirteenth sonnet, of course, there is no such pun present, but there *is* an implicit contrast with the meeker and more submissive side of the deity.

Though the imagery is not consistent in any rigorous sense, siege figures exert a binding force in the poem. God is to be (or use) a battering ram in the act of breaking down the gate of a town usurped from him. The poet's heart is the gate; and the poet is a cowed wrestler, or a defective utensil, or the besieged townspeople, or a lover forced to break troth, or a prisoner, or an unchaste person. (To bend one's force is to concentrate and direct it against specific objectives, but there are siege connotations with reference to the bending of bows, catapults, etc.) Realizing that half-way measures will have no effect, the poet begs God to liberate him forcibly from God's usurping enemy.

*Three-person'd God* is a phrase chosen with great care; it conveys in the first line an impression of triple strength for battering. In the second and fourth lines, single verbs are grouped in threes (with a fourth verb which takes a predicate); it becomes apparent that the three persons are to operate individually in this case: God the Father is to break in instead of knocking for entrance, God the Holy Spirit is to blow instead of breathing gently, and God the Son (Sun) is to burn instead of shining. (The verbs of violence alliterate with *Batter*.) Rather than seeking to mend (amend) him, God is to demolish the poet and "make me new."

Paradoxes occur throughout the poem. God is to overthrow the cowed wrestler, in order that the latter may raise and stand on his own feet. Unless God transfers the poet from the prison of sin to God's own enthrallment, the prisoner "never shall be free." And the poet will never be chaste, unless God ravishes him. It is this final paradox which strikingly combines secular and sacred love. The statement may be translated, of course, into non-erotic terms: I will never obey God's moral laws, unless he seizes me and takes me away from sin's dominion.— But the erotic implications will not expire so easily. The reference to carnal violence summarizes for us the poem's theme: that there is a sort of violence, as well as meekness, implicit in Christian doctrine. The Lamb must be complemented by the Ram.

The seventeenth sonnet alludes to secular-sacred matters, but not in any obviously startling fashion. The opening allusions refer only obliquely to physical love. Anne More has paid her last debt to nature (in death), and her last marital debt to her husband. Donne's "good" is dead—his summum bonum.—There are faintly erotic overtones in *ravish,* though carnal violence has nothing to do with the matter in this sonnet.

With the death of his wife—the payment of the last debt— Donne turns away from physical and, indeed, romantic love. His mind is wholly set on "heavenly things." The transition from one love to another has not been abrupt: love for Anne has whetted Donne's love for God. He can now see where the secular love was leading; in much the same manner do streams show their sources. The reference to water enables Donne to modulate from appetite (implicit in *whett*) to thirst. Donne has found the head of the stream, and slaked his thirst—only to have his thirst return as if he were dropsical. He has no need of begging *more* love, however: God is wooing his soul in the stead of his wife's wooing. (There may possibly be a pun on Anne's maiden name.) God is offering his own soul as a substitute for Anne's; taking the initiative in the affair, God is jealous of every potential rival—not only the Catholic's supposed worship of saints and angels, but also the secular man's worship of the world, the flesh, and the devil. The God of the Old Testament is a jealous God; here he becomes, more specifically, a jealous lover.—The Platonic ladder has led upward from love of woman to love of God.

The eighteenth sonnet, like the preceding sonnet and the

following sonnet, was first printed by Gosse, who conjectured that the three were suppressed in the seventeenth century because of their offensive Romish tendencies. Grierson adopts Gosse's argument at least partially, with reference to the eighteenth sonnet. I am unable to see why the seventeenth and the nineteenth sonnets should be offensive theologically, but the eighteenth sonnet actually *appears* too controversial for publication. If it was indeed such, the difficulty would not be (as Grierson implies) that Donne was still worrying over whether or not he had made the right decision in entering the Church of England: the difficulty would lie in Donne's independent thinking, which denied a monopoly on Christianity to any one of its major divisions. This attitude of independence was not merely transitional in Donne; it remained with him to the end, and he noted virtues and faults where he found them—in Protestantism and Catholicism alike (though his dogma was predominantly orthodox-Anglican, to the extent that orthodoxy had developed in his time).

In one of his letters Donne refers to the cramping narrowness of each of the major divisions of Christianity: "You know I never fettered nor imprisoned the word Religion; not straightning it Frierly, *ad Religiones factitias,* (as the *Romans* call well their orders of Religion) nor immuring it in a *Rome,* or a *Wittemberg,* or a *Geneva;* they are all virtuall beams of one Sun. . . . They are not so contrary as the North and South Poles. . . . Religion is Christianity, which being too spirituall to be seen by us, doth therefore take an apparent body of good life and works. . . ."[12] In the eighteenth sonnet Donne is inquiring about the true identity of Christ's spouse, the Church; the concluding implication is that Christ's spouse is not any one of the churches mentioned, but is rather a truly catholic church. There are other types of imagery present, but the imagery of secular love binds the poem together.

In the light of what follows, *Show me* of the first line has two levels of meaning. The poet wants to know the identity of Christ's spouse. He asks questions, and we can tell from the way they are phrased, that the answer to each is obviously negative: even as he asks the question, the poet realizes that he must seek further. No sensible question (let alone answer) having been forthcoming, the poet shifts to the second implication of *Show me*: If she is not any of these things mentioned, what is she? Show her to us—the spouse you have been hiding.—The poet then supplies his own answer: she is the catholic church, and Christ the husband is most pleased when he is cuckolded most.

The opening questions point up a contrast between the respective lushness and severity of Catholic and Protestant ritual. The visual contrast is that between a gaudy whore and a disheveled widow. In the questions immediately following, we are not very sharply aware of the spouse as personality. Can she sleep a thousand years, like the Catholic Church (cf. "Satyre III," line 45)—only to claim authenticity, as an *arriviste,* like the Protestant sects of the Reformation? Can she claim infallibility and yet err? Can she be subject to mutability? Is she confined to one hill (Geneva), or seven hills (Rome), or no hill (Wittenberg or Canterbury)?—The spouse becomes a woman again and the poet asks if she is present or if she is to be sought in a romantic quest. Where have you been hiding your wife?—the poet asks. We would have intercourse with her. Her fidelity is paradoxically dependent on her promiscuity. She is "most . . . pleasing to thee, then/When she'is embrac'd and open to most men."

What are the implications of Donne's mingling of secular with sacred love? They are precisely these, I think: the combiation helps Donne to show the relatedness of things (and it is more than a specious relatedness), and Donne's source of vitality is such that a mere hair's-breadth separates the erotic from the holy. We may say this, at least: Donne was no Moll Flanders who became pious on becoming too old for wickedness. Donne the voluptuous hedonist, we have said, became Donne the voluptuous saint.

5

No one can deny, I suppose, that Donne was a highly conscious artist and a highly self-conscious person (to the point of neurosis and beyond). Too much, however, has been made of the dubious assumption that he was a highly self-conscious artist. He was hardly Romantic (either upper or lower case) enough to think of himself as primarily a poet—to engage in the absurdity of Life for Art's Sake. Indeed, the unique quality of his poetry is attributable primarily to the fact that he was no esthetic sissy. It was not merely to be different or to be fashionable that he crammed scientific imagery (for example) into his poems: he was intertested in what was going on around him, and scientific investigation was all the rage. Scientific imagery had been all the rage, too,[13] but Donne's interest survived the fad.

No one of course, has accused Donne of being a *fin de siècle* esthete. (Oddly enough, Arthur Symons, who *might* so be accused, has commented on Donne's many-sided interests.)[14] But the tendency is still current—despite the efforts of Miss Rosemond Tuve—to consider him the leader of a revolt against the prevailing mode of poetry in his time. And Mr. Brooks has led us to think of Donne as aware of ironies within ironies within ironies—all presumably conceived by Donne to justify himself to future generations of literary critics.

Mr. Brooks's theory is not based solely on his analysis of "The Canonization": he also cites the Window valediction. with reference to the "cleansing" of metaphor.[15] This valediction represents one variety of Donne's multiple-choice technique. Like a dog with a bone, he worries a basic figure until there is nothing more it can do for him. Unlike the dog's, his worrying is purposive—not in the least irresponsible. Learning is not displayed for its own sake here, though a superficial reading might lead us to that conclusion. The basic material of the poem is a name inscribed on a windowpane. First it symbolizes the speaker's fidelity to his beloved—a relationship which has nothing to conceal. Then this metaphor (or, rather, series of metaphors) is partially repudiated, in favor of a new series: the name is to represent the speaker's mortal remains; his lady's constant grief can eventually repair the ravages of death resulting from absence. A further shift in tone occurs here, when the speaker imagines a scene of potential betrayal; the name is to exert a sort of magical influence, to protect his interests. But the greatest shift in tone of all, occurs in the final stanza, in which all the preceding imagery is apparently discarded as invalid: this has all been delirious raving, since the name is inadequate as a symbol.

The final stanza picks up a figure used implicitly in one of the earlier alternatives: the notion that absence from his beloved constitutes death for the lover. This circumstance gives Mr. Brooks an opportunity to generalize on poetic theory. The rejection of the earlier alternatives might seem to indicate rejection of the figures as fantastic, monstrous, far-fetched. But no sooner has this rejection occurred, than the very same sort of language is used to explain the error of judgment. The implication would be that only through such language—fantastic though it may seem, to the uninitiated—can complex poetic statements of this type, be made with any adequacy.

Mr. Brooks uses this argument to support his thesis about wit and high seriousness in poetry. [16] With this thesis I agree in general, but I feel that in this instance he has weakened his case by an unhappy choice of material to support his point. Regarding "the repudiation-of-the-repudiation" at the end of the poem, Mr. Brooks notes that the effect

> . . . is not to end the poem on a note of mere flippancy. On the contrary, the effect is to justify the poet's use of wit here as an adequate—and in this experience, at least, an inevitable—instrument. We may describe the effect somewhat clumsily as follows: the poet is conscious of the fantastic nature of his development of the original conceit, but having indicated his awareness of this, can only brazen out the fantasy; or, he would tell his mistress what he wishes to tell her in sober statement, not in "idle talk," if he could, but, having considered the possibility, he can, after all, make use of no better instrument than his original metaphorical language. The poem, then, may be said to carry within itself an ironical justification of the method which it employs.[17]

True, metaphorical language *does* permit us to combine wit and high seriousness, and no one has succeeded better in the attempt than Donne at his best. I find it inconceivable, however, that anyone fresh from a reading of the Donne canon, could attribute Mr. Brooks's implication to Donne. As we have noted, Donne never seems self-conscious or apologetic about what we sometimes consider the fantastic element in his imagery. He is not apologizing in this valediction. Essentially, the talk is idle, not because it employs absurd imagery, but because distrust of the lady is absurd (there is some irony in the speaker's statement here). In rejecting Mr. Brooks's reading, we may be forced to conclude that Donne's final stanza is a little lame. So be it; there *are* sympathetic critics who find Donne's poems uneven in quality. The case in this poem seems to be one simply of the multiple-choice device which exhausts all posibilities in choice, and then proceeds to explore the further possibility that these potentialities never really existed.

In a sense, the speaker of the poem is whittling down his

claim, in successive stages. The name, for example, will make the lady "As much more loving, as more sad," in his absence—yet the speaker immediately considers a situation in which the lady is at least potentially unfaithful. Of course, the name's magical power will take care of the situation, but if it doesn't, it will take care of the further situation that develops—and so on. To repeat, the multiple-choice device exhausts all possibilities in choice, and then proceeds to explore the further possibility that these potentialities never existed at all. In Donne the rejection of an alternative never really cancels out anything. The basic fluctuation in this valediction is that between trust and distrust of the lady. The final stanza tends to give us the impression that the relationship rests on the sound basis of mutual love, but there is still floating around in the background the idea that betrayal is not impossible.

In an age of great poets, Donne seems to have been acquainted intimately with only one poet of first importance—Ben Jonson. (Donne also knew, however, the talented sons of his friend Lady Herbert.) He was an omnivorous reader, yet we find him writing (perhaps to Sir Henry Wotton):

. . . I am no great voyager in other mens works: no swallower nor devowrer of volumes nor pursuant of authors. Perchaunce it is because I find borne in my self knowledg or apprehension enough[,] for (without forfeiture or impeachment of modesty) I think I am bond to god thankfully to acknowledg it) [comma needed instead of parenthesis?] to consyder him [God] & my self: as [,] when I haue at home a convenient garden [,] I covet not to walk in others broad medows or woods [,] especially because it falls not within that short reach which my foresight embraceth to see how I should employ that which I already know [;] to travayle for inquiry of more were to labor to gett a stomach & then find no meat at home. To know how to liue by the booke is a pedantery, & to do it is a bondage. [comma needed instead of period?] for both hearers & players are more delighted with voluntary then with sett musike.[18]

The application of this passage to his own poetry, was probably not in Donne's intention, but his basic attitude leads us to believe that his poems were written neither in imitation of nor in revolt against contemporary poetic fashions. It is perhaps beside the point, but Donne seldom even alludes to the fashionable theme of poetry as immortalizing; when he does, it is always with a difference. In the Book valediction it is the quality of the lovers' experience—and not poetry (even in the broad sense)—which actually immortalizes the book of their love. While Donne reminds Lady Bedford ("This twilight of two yeares, not past nor next . . .") that "Verse embalmes vertue" (l. 13), he also notes that his own verses "are short-liv'd" (l. 16). All this, of course, must be taken in the context of Donne's eulogy of Lady Bedford; his personal attitude is not necessarily revealed. The same may be said for the allusion at the end of *An Anatomie of the World*. The fourth epistle "To Mr. T. W." ("At once, from hence, my lines and I depart . . .") contains a reference to verse as perdurable though perhaps not as immortalizing.—We would be unwise to conclude that Donne had no interest in his verse's chances of survival, but he is relatively unconcerned—explicitly, if not implicitly—with the theme of immortality through verse.

For reasons which are somewhat obscure to us (apart from his added vulnerability to attack), Donne regretted—after the appearance of the *Anniversaries*—having "descended to print any thing in verse."[19] He evidently enjoyed having his poems circulate in manuscript, but was not imprudent enough to wish them in print. Just before taking Orders, he felt for a time—with whatever reluctance—the necessity of collecting his poems in book form "as a valediction to the world." "By this occasion," he writes Sir Henry Goodyere, "I am made a Rhapsoder of mine own rags, and that cost me more diligence, to seek them, then it did to make them."[29] (He is rounding up copies of his poems.) The cavalier attitude towards the importance of keeping copies and towards the labor of composition, probably supports my thesis about Donne's lack of self-consciousness, though at this stage of his life Donne would naturally disparage his poems because of their pagan implications. In Donne's time there *was,* of course, the convention that gentlemen did not publish their literary works, unless corrupt transcriptions or pirated editions forced them to do so.[21] Donne's reluctance to publish cannot be offered as conclusive evidence that he was or was not a self-conscious artist. At most, the reluctance indicates that he was a man of his age.

Allen R. Benham conjectures that Donne "was nauseated by the conventional current poetry."[22] Benham's note refers to "Satyre II" and to the letter "To Mr. Rowland Woodward" ("Like one who'in her third widdowhood doth professe . . ."). Let us examine these poems for evidence of possible nausea. "Satyre II" is a savage attack directed primarily against the greed represented by the lawyer and onetime-poetaster Coscus —perhaps a composite of persons despised by Donne or by the indignant speaker of the poem. In law the ethical practices of Coscus are detestable, whether or not the same was true of his poetic career. At any rate, there is satire here of a sort of hierarchy of poetasters, of which the plagiarist is the worst—the uninspired playwright, for example, or the amateur of both poetry and love, or the sycophantic beggar in verse, or the dilettantish faddist. It is difficult to believe that Donne—if he *is* speaking in his own person—could have mistaken these charlatans for the typical practitioners of poetry in his own time. This passage is primarily social, rather than literary, criticism.

In the epistle to Woodward, Donne refers to his muse as having shown "to few, yet to too many . . . /How love-song weeds, and Satyrique thornes are growne/Where seeds of better Arts, were early sown" (ll. 4-6). Mr. Benham evidently con siders this a reference to the state of poetry in Donne's time. (Even if it were, it would not be universally damning.) But the context indicates that *my muse* refers to Donne's private muse—not merely to the muse of poetry. The "better Arts" here seem to be those pertaining to religion; tares (love-songs and satires) have grown up to choke out the wheat (hymns, perhaps). Donne's poems had had a limited audience, but too many people had seen them for his own peace of mind at this juncture.

There are other passages, however, which seem more specifically satirical. Donne's letter "To the Countesse of Salisbury" notes that the sun, "Growne stale, is to so low a value runne, /That his disshevel'd beames and scattered fires/Serve but for Ladies Periwigs and Tyres/In lovers Sonnets. . . ." (Ll. 4-7.) There may indeed be a sly dig here at the uninspired imagery of lover-boy poets, but the really important effect is that of irony. As the context reveals, the universe is all out of kilter. The sun has been degraded to a position of minor importance (the new philosophy calls in doubt) : logically, then, women's wigs—instead of their eyes, as formerly—are being compared with the sun.

In the Lesbian seduction poem, "Heroicall Epistle: Sapho to Philaenis," there is a passage which is—at first sight—strongly reminiscent of Shakespeare's "Sonnet 130." Shakespeare's down-to-earth sonnet ridicules imagery comparing a lady's eyes to the sun, for example. His (Shakespeare's or the speaker's) conclusion is that his mistress, who could never qualify under such conditions, is actually as attractive as women who *are* so described. Here, for comparsion, is the passage in Donne (Sappho addressing Philaenis) :

Thou art not so soft, and cleare, and strait, and faire

As *Downe,* as *Stars, Cedars,* and *Lillies* are,
But thy right hand, and cheek, and eye, only
Are like thy other hand, and cheek, and eye.
(Ll. 21-24.)

The implication in Donne is entirely different from that in
Shakespeare. The comparison is invalid between eyes and stars
(say), not because the idea is ridiculous, but simply because
stars afford a very inept approximation to the eyes' brightness.
We may check this conclusion with the context of the passage;
the same hyperbole obtains, a few line above: " . . . Thou art so
faire,/As *gods,* when *gods* to thee I doe compare,/Are grac'd
thereby. . . ." (Ll. 15-17.) (There may, of course, be incidental
satire in the thoroughly predictable discarded-comparisons—eyes
with stars, etc.)

Thomas Carew, more or less a disciple of Donne's, offers
evidence which might be taken to support a position contrary to
mine. In his elegy on Donne, Carew credits his master with
(among other things) leading poetry away from idol worship.
The idols are the gods of anicent mythology, and their worship
has been accompanied by a honey-tongued mellifluousness. Here
are the pertinent passages:

Thou shalt yield no precedence, but of time
And the blinde fate of language, whose tun'd chime
More charmes the outward sense; yet thou maist claime
From so great disadvantage greater fame,
Since to the awe of thy imperious wit
Our stubborn language bends, made only fit
With her tough-rib'd hoopes to gird about
Thy Giant phansie, which had prov'd too stout
For their soft melting Phrases . . . .

\* \* \*

. . . Thou art gone, and thy strict lawes will be
Too hard for Libertines in Poetrie.
They will repeale the goodly exil'd traine

Of gods and goddesses, which in thy just raigne  
Were banish'd nobler Poems, now, with these  
The silenc'd tales o'th'Metamorphoses  
Shall stuffe their lines, and swell the windy Page,  
Till Verse refin'd by thee, in this last Age,  
Turne ballad rime, Or those old Idolls bee  
Ador'd againe, with new apostasie. . . .

(Ll. 45-53 and 61-70; see Grierson, I, 379.)

Far from hanging him (according to Ben Jonson's suggestion), Carew is ready to canonize Donne for not keeping accent. Donne is not the libertine; his laws are strict, and he has altered intractable language to express his original thoughts. Soft melting phrases are good enough for servile imitators, but Donne has made a break with tradition.

These observations look very much like hindsight. Carew's poem, we must remember, was an elegy—written some time between Donne's death in 1631, and the publication of the 1633 edition. Carew was not so devoted a disciple of Donne's that he discarded classical mythology himself; he could well have been mistaken about, for example, Donne's neglecting such allusions as a matter of policy (rather than as a matter of predilection). Whether or not the break with tradition was as clean and premeditated as it seemed to Carew in retrospect, by Donne's death (at least), the uniqueness of the movement he started—however inadvertently—must have seemed sufficiently evident.

Even during Donne's lifetime, Ben Jonson seems to have realized that Donne's poetry was set apart, in certain respects, from the conventional poetry of the time. That Donne himself was acutely aware of this difference, is another and more dangerous assumption. Jonson's comments have survived only in the record of his conversations with William Drummond of Hawthornden. In Drummond's paraphrase, the comments sound epigrammatic, and hence too sweepingly arbitrary to be altogether just.

Of Jonson's observations on Donne, the most pertinent here are the following three:

That Done, for not keeping of accent, deserved hanging.[23]

That Done said to him we wrott that Epitaph on Prince Henry, Look to me, Fath, to match Sir Ed: Herbert in obscureness.[24]

That Done himself, for not being understood, would perish.[25]

Jonson's own verse sometimes seems to us harsh, if not obscure. Unfortunately, we have no information on the precise grounds for his censure of Donne, and we cannot say whether this criticism was delivered directly to Donne. *Understood,* in the third comment, is rather ambiguous; it may not refer to characteristic obscurity at all, but—in the sense of *appreciated*—merely to the limited appeal which Donne's poetry might be expected to have. (The word *Understanders* is perenially misinterpreted in the prefatory "The Printer to the Understanders." The printer of Donne's poems is addressing the "discerner"; he is not being sarcastic about Donne's obscurity.) As Patterson's edition of the *Conversations* indicates, Jonson *did* consider Donne too difficult for beginners in poetry.

The second comment is relatively concrete. Donne's remark however, may merely have been a playful commentary on Lord Herbert's obscurity. In terms of the so-called "Metaphysical School," the master here seems to be imitating the pupil, if Donne is to be taken seriously.—This comment is hardly valid evidence that Donne deliberately cultivated an obscure style. At least three of his poems seem to be obscure by design, but the "Nocturnall," "Twicknam garden," and "Satyre II" are special cases: Donne evidently prefers not to have the reader associate them with his private life.

Drummond notes that "To me [Jonson] read the preface of his Arte of Poesie, upon Horace Arte of Poesie, wher he heth ane Apologie of a play of his, St. Bartholomees Faire, by Criticus is understood Done."[26] In a later passage, Drummond repeats this statement: "[Jonson] hath commented and translated Horace Art of Poesie: it is in dialogue wayes; by Criticus he understandeth Dr Done."[27] Jonson's preface has not been preserved, and hence no more than speculation is possible, on the meaning of Drummond's statement. Presumably, Jonson's commentary on Horace is in dialogue-form, and the character of Criticus represents Donne and presents Donne's views on poetry. Herford and Simpson characterize Jonson's preface as "a defence for a deviation from the norm of 'art'—his rough-and-tumble comedy of *Bartholomew Fair*."[28] If Jonson's editors are right, poetry in the broad sense must have been under discussion, since *Bartholomew Fair* is not even in verse. At any rate, we are hardly justified in assuming that Donne as Criticus delivered a credo of Metaphysical poetry.

I have not tried to demonstrate that Donne could have had no codifiable views on poetry: I have merely tried to show that Donne was not acutely conscious of occupying the historical position now commonly assigned him—that of an iconoclast in revolt against Petrarchanism.

# *Lightness Depresseth Us*

THE TITLE OF this chapter is taken from a line in Donne's third verse-letter to Lady Bedford ("T'have written then . . ."). In context, "Lightness depresseth us" is paired off with "emptiness fills"—the two paradoxes expressing dissatisfaction with the ills of Donne's time. Using Dr. Donne's own methods of textual explication, we may consider ways in which this text might have a wider applicability than its context alone would warrant.

In the poems to be dealt with in this chapter, we find a mood of profound depression. With reference to one of these poems, our title might be applied with punning effect: Lightness (consorting with light women) depresseth us (physically and psychically). The other two poems join this one in contrasting sharply with the prevailing tone of the Songs and Sonnets group: a lightness of touch which can convey thematic material ranging from Petrarchan adoration to cynical distrust of womankind. The poems of this chapter seem almost to react against such lightness of mood—without, however, necessarily representing any sort of palinode or anticipation of Donne's later reaction to the secular love poems. At any rate, in this summarizing chapter we must commit ourselves on the problem of sex and high seriousness in Donne—this problem being central to a final evaluation of the body of Donne's poetry.

2
### A nocturnall upon S. Lucies day,
### Being the shortest day

Tis the yeares midnight and it is the dayes,
*Lucies,* who scarce seaven houres herself unmaskes,
    The Sunne is spent, and now his flasks
    Send forth light squibs, no constant rays:
5        The worlds whole sap is sunke:
The generall balme th'hydroptique earth hath drunk,
Whither, as to the beds-feet, life is shrunke,
Dead and enterr'd; yet all these seeme to laugh,
Compar'd with mee, who am their Epitaph.

10   Study me then, you who shall lovers bee
At the next world, that is, at the next Spring:
    For I am every dead thing,
    In whom love wrought new Alchemie.
      For his art did expresse
15 A quintessence even from nothingnesse,
From dull privations, and leane emptinesse
He ruin'd mee, and I am re-begot
Of absence, darknesse, death; things which are not.

All others, from all things, draw all that's good,
20   Life, soule, forme, spirit, whence they beeing have;
    I, by loves limbecke, am the grave
    Of all, that's nothing. Oft a flood
      Have wee two wept, and so
Drownd the whole world, us two; oft did we grow
25 To be two Chaosses, when we did show
Care to ought else; and often absences
Withdrew our soules, and made us carcasses.

But I am by her death, (which word wrongs her)
Of the first nothing, the Elixir grown;
30     Were I a man, that I were one,
    I needs must know; I should preferre,
      If I were any beast,

Some ends, some means; Yea plants, yea stones detest,
And love; All, all some properties invest;
35 If I an ordinary nothing were,
As shadow, a light, and body must be here.
But I am None; nor will my Sunne renew.
You lovers, for whose sake, the lesser Sunne
At this time to the Goat is runne
40 To fetch new lust, and give it you,
Enjoy your summer all,
Since shee enjoyes her long nights festivall,
Let mee prepare towards her, and let mee call
This houre her Vigill, and her Eve, since this
45 Both the yeares, and the dayes deep midnight is.

Critics have tended, for two reasons, to regard this poem as
addressed to Lucy, Countess of Bedford: first, the name *Lucy*
appears in the poem and the title; and, second, a poem of this
intensity and "sincerity" must obviously (according their view)
have been founded on a specific personal experience. The second
reason, as I have repeatedly tried to point out with reference to
the biographical and the sinceritas heresies, is more than suspect
as a basis for procedure. And the first reason, alone, can justify
only further investigation of the internal evidence in the poem,
and of the external evidence bearing directly on the poem. I believe that such evidence, in this case, points towards a personal
experience. External evidence—such as is available—would seem
to support the conclusion towards which the internal evidence
points.

No critic seems to have been particularly troubled by the
wording of the poem's title. At least one editor has commented
that, in Donne's time, St. Lucy's Day was the shortest day of the
year—a piece of research based solely on the reading of Donne's
title. According to the Julian calendar, St. Lucy's Day fell on
13 December—the same day every year—while the "shortest" day
of the year varied periodically. In his selected edition, Garrod

comments that the two days could not possibly have coincided during Donne's lifetime, but Garrod is strangely uncurious about Donne's motives for juxtaposing the two in his title. As a matter of fact, Garrod's statement—as well as his judgment—is inconclusive, since his statement is based on scientific computation: the important fact is not what modern scientists *know* was the shortest day of a particular year in a particular region, but what the English people living at that time *thought* the shortest day. The significant evidence must come from the almanacs published during Donne's lifetime.

The critic may prove the invalidity of Garrod's statement, simply by referring to the almanac published by Richard Allestree for the year 1626. This almanac lists 13 December as the shortest day of the year. There is no good reason, however, for attaching Donne's poem to 1626, and it is unlikely that the two days coincided during the actual year of composition. (I make the latter statement on the basis of those almanacs I have been able to examine, directly or indirectly—most of them for the period, somewhat earlier than 1626, in which the poem was presumably written.—Miss Marlies Kallman generously interrupted her own research at the British Museum to supplement my information on the almanacs of Donne's time.)

Why, then, would Donne speak of St. Lucy's Day as the shortest day of the year?—Perhaps he was using approximate terms. In *Of the Progresse of the Soule,* line 120, a St. Lucy's night is used to symbolize a long but finite period for the sleep of Elizabeth Drury's soul. No claim is made, however, that St. Lucy's Day is neccessarily the shortest day of the year: St. Lucy's is simply the longest night identifiable with a name. It is rather unlikely that Donne should be using approximate terms in the nocturnal. One of the major points of the poem is that the speaker's emotional depression coincides precisely with nature's lowest seasonal ebb. But this depression is connected with St.

Lucy's Day, which must actually have *followed* the point of lowest ebb. It is hard to believe that Donne would abandon his naturalistic substructure after adhering to it so closely.

Why might not the name St. Lucy refer, not (or not merely) to the ecclesiastical saint, but to a saint in love's religion? There would seem to be a personal reference here to Lucy, Countess of Bedford, as dying (in some qualified sense) on the shortest day of the year in which the poem was written. How does Grierson's hypothesis fit this picture?—Grierson offers, with some hesitation, the conjecture that the poem might have been written in 1612 on the occasion of the seemingly-mortal illness of Lady Bedford (see Grierson, II, 10). Grierson is somewhat reluctant to believe Lucy the subject of this poem, because part of the poem "speaks a stronger language than that of Petrarchian adoration."

In 1612, the shortest day of the year was (thought to be) 12 December. Had it been 11 December, we might have rejected Grierson's hypothesis on this basis alone, since Donne seems to be setting up a complex counterpoint between the day of the secular St. Lucy, and that—immediately following—of the sacred St. Lucy. "This houre," the midnight of the secular St. Lucy's Day, is both "her [St. Lucy Secular's] Vigill, and her [St. Lucy Sacred's] Eve" (both the Vigil and the Eve precede an actual feast day). As the year's midnight (the point of lowest ebb), the hour might be Lucy Bedford's Vigil—a period of watching, and praying for her soul; or it might be the Vigil preceding the ecclesiastical St. Lucy's Day. Similarly, as the day's midnight, the hour might be St. Lucy's Eve in the ecclesiastical sense, or Lucy Bedford's eve to a new life (the word *death* wrongs her).

But Grierson's hypothesis assumes, without supporting evidence, that Lucy Bedford's historically documented illness of late November, 1612, had not passed the critical stage by mid-December, and that "Donne may have written in anticipation of her death." However pessimistic a person may be about a loved one's chances of survival, the former is likely to hope against hope—to abandon hope only when the medical evidence is final. If Donne had received an erroneous report of Lady Bedford's death, the fact would surely have been recorded somewhere.

My own hypothesis is that the poem was written in 1594 on the occasion of Lucy Harington's marriage to Edward Russell, third Earl of Bedford. The poem is by no means an epithalamium; few poets would be cheerful enough to write an epithalamium for a wedding in which they had vainly hoped to be the bridegroom. I have no biographical support for this conclusion; most commentators believe that it was more than a dozen years before Donne even met Lucy. There are simply no definite biographical facts available to us now, to establish the time of their meeting. We know that Lucy was very young—not quite fourteen—in 1594, but she seems to have been quite mature for her age, and we have no reason to suspect that the marriage was merely nominal.[1] (It might be noted that Donne was approximately the same age as her bridegroom, that Donne later chose a wife some years younger than he, and that Elizabeth Drury—when she died at the age of fifteen—was hardly thought of as the child we like to consider her.) R. C. Bald's forthcoming biography of Donne may prove this hypothesis untenable, but the combination of internal and external evidence strongly indicates (to my view) that the hypothesis is worth considering.

In order to explain specifically what I think this poem is about, I should like to reconstruct the poem (in part) conjecturally. My reconstruction will be highly mechanical, of course; I will hardly insist that Donne followed the precise sequence I am about to suggest, or that all this occurred in Donne's conscious mind during the process of composition. I merely want to indicate what (according to my view) Donne had to work with, and what he did with it.—On 12 December Lucy became the Countess of Bedford (this is an historical fact). In 1594 this was (believed to be) the shortest day of the year. The new day beginning at midnight was St. Lucy's Day, 13 December. Donne started out with these facts, plus their implications—chief of which was the profound depression of spirits in which Lucy's marriage had left him.

Donne had before him a ready-made correlation between the microcosm and the macrocosm: at this time of year nature, like his own spirits, was at an ebb. Spring would provide a regeneration for nature, but there the similarity no longer held true. What potentialities did St. Lucy's Day offer?—First of all, on the obvious level, it duplicated the name of the woman he had reverenced as a saint in love's religion. There are further implications in the name of the saint: W. A. Murray puts the matter thus: " . . . St. Lucie . . . here appears as a saint of light (*lux.*), and hence associated quite normally with the shortest day (death or martyrdom of light). . . ."[2] (This pun on the name *Lucy* has no particular relevance to the history of the ecclesiastical St. Lucy. With reference to Lady Bedford, this very pun on the name *Lucy* occurs in Ben Jonson's "To Lucy, Countesse of of Bedford, with M. Donnes Satyres"; see Grierson, I, 6. There *may* be implicit puns of this type in Donne's verse-letters to Lady Bedford.) There is thus potential irony in the term *Day*—irony echoed in the phrase *shortest day*, which appears in the title of the poem. Notice that *day* is used in two slightly different (and perfectly conventional) senses, in the title: St. Lucy's Day is the period of 24 hours which is otherwise designated 13 December, whereas (according to popular usage) the shortest day of any year is not one which falls short of 24 hours, but the one which has the shortest period between sunrise and sunset. The second *day* is more the antithesis of night, than it is the measure of time.

At any rate, the Day of St. Lucy Russell is virtually 70 per-
cent night. Her day really begins when she goes to bed on her
wedding night. Night is day for her, and this fact provides
Donne with some ironies poignant to him: " . . . She enjoys her
long nights festivall," while he is agonizing over his loss. "Let
mee prepare towards her," he says, in the language of the bridegroom anticipating the consummation of marriage—but Donne
can only prepare to do reverence to St. Lucy Martyr. "This
houre" is St. Lucy Russell's "Vigill"; Donne's watching and
praying is due to the sleeplessness and anguish her marriage has
caused him, while *she* is keeping vigil (remaining awake) for a
different purpose. The Church's St. Lucy is designated Virgin
and Martyr; St. Lucy Russell is a martyr because she is no longer
a virgin. This is "her Eve," the prelude to a new life after her
erotic death as virgin. As we have noted, the year's shortest day
is appropriate for the martyrdom of the Church's St. Lucy as
Light, and of Donne's own St. Lucy as Virgin. Cf. ll. 49f. of
the Lincoln's Inn epithalamium: " . . . Winter dayes bring much
delight,/Not for themselves, but for they soon bring night. . . ."
Cf. also ll. 83f. of the Valentine epithalamium: "Let not this
day, then, but this night be thine,/Thy day was but the eve to
this, O Valentine."

The reference to the sun, in the first stanza, is seasonal: the
sun, of course, is hardly visible at midnight—even in the feeble
appearance described. The sun, *whenever* it appears during this
season, sends forth only lightly-charged bursts from its powder
flasks. In terms of trees, the sap of the world has sunk. In Par-
acelsian terms, the universal balsam has sunk back into the earth,
its matrix.[3] It is as if a dying man's vital forces had seeped
downward through the pillars of the bed on which he was lying.
But all the manifestations of death in nature "seeme to laugh,"
compared with the poet: by comparison they show signs not
only of life but of vivacity, while the poet is only their somber

epitaph—he survives all these manifestations, only to outdo them in dying.

Love has wrought a new kind of alchemy in the poet: a quintessential nothingness, surpassing that which formerly obtained, when he and his beloved quarreled, drowning their private world in tears (cf. the Weeping valediction); or when their unified world fell apart into two chaoses, as the result of a breach in fidelity; or when, in physical absence, their souls were stretched out between their tenantless bodies.

The new nothingness is traceable to the death of the beloved —death in a qualified sense: the "word wrongs her," since this is a death into new vitality, the martyrdom of virginity. If the poet were a human being, his characteristic reason would so assure him; if he were an animal, he would still have some power of choice; even plants and stones have some faculty of attraction and repulsion. But the poet is still lower in the Great Chain of Being. If he were even a shadow, an ordinary nothing, that would presuppose a light and a physical body of some type—but he is all darkness and nothingness.

The poet's sun will not renew her benevolent beaming. We have a contrast, then, between this sun and "the lesser Sunne" of the physical world, whose entrance into the astronomical sign Capricorn has marked this as the shortest day of the year. For other lovers, the winter will dissipate with spring; even now, the sun has gone to the Goat (Capricorn) "To fetch new lust" for them. Let them enjoy their short summer nights: the poet's St. Lucy is even now (to adapt a line from "Loves Alchymie") enjoying a summer-seeming winter's night. The cruel irony of the situation is that for Donne it is a winter-seeming winter's night—this product of his dreaming "a rich and long delight."

The punctuation of line 41 is a matter of crucial importance to my reading. Here is Grierson on this line: "The old editions have a comma [for which Grierson substitutes a semicolon].

Chambers, obviously quite wrongly, retains the comma, and
closes the sentence in the next line. The clause 'Since she enjoys
her long night's festival' explains 43 'Let me prepare towards
her,' &c., not 41 'Enjoy your summer all.' " Chambers and Grierson are equally wrong in adopting an either-or attitude: line 42
works both ways, and explains both line 41 and line 43. The
ambiguous value of an Elizabethan comma (anywhere from a
very slight pause to very nearly a full stop), makes certain passages intractable to modernized punctuation.[4] Grierson's emendation would rob this passage of the parallelism between *Enjoy*
and *enjoyes,* and the contrast between short and long nights
of festivity. Chambers's emendation, of course, robs the passage
of its continuity. The fact that St. Lucy is enjoying "her long
nights festivall," causes Donne (in fancy) to prepare to do
reverence to *one* St. Lucy, and—ironically, as we have noted—
to prepare for bedding down with *the other* St. Lucy.

## 3
### Twicknam garden

> Blasted with sighs, and surrounded with teares,
>     Hither I come to seeke the spring,
>     And at mine eyes, and at mine ears,
> Receive such balmes, as else cure every thing;
>     But O, selfe traytor, I do bring
> The spider love, which transubstantiates all,
>     And can convert Manna to gall,
> And that this place may thoroughly be thought
>     True Paradise, I have the serpent brought.
>
> 10  'Twere wholsomer for mee, that winter did
>     Benight the glory of this place,
>     And that a grave frost did forbid
> These trees to laugh, and mocke mee to my face;
>     But that I may not this disgrace
> 15  Indure, nor yet I leave loving, Love let mee

## Lightness Depresseth Us

>Some senslesse peece of this place bee;
>>Make me a mandrake, so I may groane here,
>>>Or a stone fountaine weeping out my yeare.

>Hither with christall vyals, lovers come,
>>And take my tears, which are loves wine,
>>>And try your mistresse Tears at home,
>For all are false, that tast not just like mine;
>>Alas, hearts do not in eyes shine,
>Nor can you more judge womans thoughts by teares,
>>Then by her shadow, what she weares.
>O perverse sexe, where none is true but shee,
>>Who's therefore true, because her truth kills mee.

20 marks line 20 at "And take my tears, which are loves wine,"

"Twicknam garden" has been identified with Lady Bedford, for much the same reasons which obtained in the case of the "Nocturnall." The lady lived in Twicknam Park, the poem is obviously "sincere" (by popular belief) and hence personal, and—moreover—its tone appears to resemble that of the "Nocturnall," with the latter's asumed ties to Lady Bedford. Of these reasons I would accept only the first as valid—and that only to the extent that more positive evidence is forthcoming upon investigation. The title refers to a specific physical locale—a fact which occurs in the case of no other among the dramatic (as opposed to manifestly public or personal) poems, with the possible exception of "The Primrose" (a controversial case at best). It is rather unlikely that Donne could have had any acquaintance with Twickenham Park apart from his acquaintance with Lady Bedford.

Despite the unusual nature of the title, the poem may very well be based on an imaginary situation. Or, even if it is not, the personal reference may be—not to Lady Bedford—but to some feminine member of Lady Bedford's literary court at Twickenham Park. If we consider this an actual incident, we must be prepared to abandon the common belief that Donne never looked at another woman, after his marriage to Anne More. I am myself quite willing to abandon this belief as sentimental and oversimplified, but "Twicknam garden" offers no conclusive evidence against the belief.

The word *spring,* in the second line of the poem, bears heavy concepual weight on three levels: as the season spring, as the figurative therapeutic waters, and as—above all—the source ("so streames do show their head"—to quote "Holy Sonnet XVII"). Blasted by a wintry gale of (his own) sighs, and overflowed by a freshet of tears, the speaker comes to Twickenham Park to seek a more balmy climate, to seek the "head" of these sighs and tears, and to seek the healing powers of the spring "at mine eyes" ("surrounded with teares") and "at mine eares" ("Blasted with sighs"). The reference to "such balmes, as else cure every thing" anticipates the failure of the mission. Presumably the lady's benign countenance and soothing voice, remarkable as their powers are, could effect cures in any circumstances other than these, for absence from the lady has caused the maladies. But the speaker, a "selfe traytor," has brought love—not merely admiration—with him. Love, in this setting, is a spider whose poison taints everything.—Notice how Donne builds up to a comparison of this garden with the Garden of Eden: first, there is the ecclesiastical term *transubstantiates,* then the Bibical reference to manna, and finally the ironic allusion to "True Paradise," complete with serpent. The speaker's love has no business here.

In the "Nocturnall" the speaker's depression was heightened by juxtaposition with the seasonal ebb of nature. Here there is an ironic contrast between the speaker's winter and nature's spring; the cheerful vitality of the trees seems to mock him. A "grave" (1. heavy; 2. staid and sober) frost would remedy matters, but frosts are out of season. The speaker could avoid the disgrace of mockery, by desisting from love, which causes his depression of spirits. But he is unwilling to take such a course of action. There is another alternative, and he begs love to make him "Some senslesse [i.e., non-rational] peece of this place." He prefers an existence as a mandrake, whose habit of groaning would keep the lover's groans inconspicuous—or as a stone fountain, whose incessant weeping would coincide with the lover's own.

The speaker then fancies that he has in fact become a fountain from which tears are flowing. His tears, the distillation of love, constitute a sort of wine; he states categorically that his tears are an index to genuine grief. Other lovers, then, may use the wine of his tears as a criterion in testing the vintage of their own ladies' tears. In themselves, the latter tears are hardly a certain indication of women's grief, at a time of parting.—The concluding couplet of the poem presents major difficulties in interpretation, most of which hinge on the implications of *true* and *truth*. There are two senses in which *true* may be applied to the speaker's comment on women's tears: We can't tell whether such tears are true (i.e., genuine) expressions of deep emotion; hence we can't tell whether the women wil be true (i. e, faithful) to us.

We may try these values in the concluding couplet: "O perverse sexe, where none is true [truth-telling; faithful] but shee,/ Who's therefore true, because her truth [truth-telling; fidelity] kills mee. " Using one value at a time, we get these two statements (which ultimately amount to the same statement): 1. The only truth-telling person in the female sex, is the particular woman I love—and *she* kills me by telling me truthfully that she doesn't love me (the second value of *true*. applies even here: she is serving my best interests by telling me the truth directly, however much it hurts; in this sense she is faithful to me [there may also be the implication that the speaker, by his behavior, is being unfaithful to someone else, as well as demanding infidelity on the part of the woman addressed (cf. "Loves Deitie"): the lady he loves would serve his best interests by squelching his pretensions at once]); 2. The only faithful person in the female sex, is the particular person I love—and *she* kills me by being faithful to another man (she is also in a sense truth-telling: her behavior gives me no reason to believe that I have a chance).

The wording of the last line introduces special difficulties. The lady is "therefore true, because her truth kills mee." *Therefore* is simply anticipatory of a reason to follow; *because* is the perplexing word: it implies that the lady is true simply to spite the speaker. I doubt that this implication is valid, but suspect that Donne deliberately introduced a hint of malice-aforethought, in order to strengthen his characterization of woman as a perverse sex. Actually, *because her truth kills mee* seems to mean only *in the sense that her particular type of "truth" kills me* (*instead of completing my happiness*).

Even if this poem were proved incontrovertibly the product of Donne's personal acquaintance with (and postulated love for) Lady Bedford, we would be justified in drawing only a limited number of conclusions from it. Sexual seduction would not necessarily have been in question at all. Donne might merely have been asking Lucy to turn back the clock to a time when they appeared to be mutually in love. We would have no reason for assuming that love was not involved in Donne's marriage to Anne More. Renewed acquaintance with Lady Bedford—with Lucy this time as a generous patroness of arts—might have revived in Donne an infatuation (if such ever existed) which he had thought quite dead. Donne's wife, of course, was hardly set off to advantage by a home of financial straits, of an ever-increasing brood of babies, and of isolation from court intrigues, fashions, and intellectual pursuits. Lady Bedford represented virtually the opposite, to Donne. The poem's sweeping reference to woman's infidelity, would hardly have to apply to Anne Donne, of course. Donne would presumably be ignoring her existence for the time, and trying to recapture a mutual relationship which may have existed in his own mind only.

Grierson informs us that the "Nocturnall" is to be found in no extant manuscript collection dated earlier than Lady Bedford's death. If the fact is significant—and it may not be so—it would seem to indicate an unwillingness on Donne's part, for her sake and his, to have a warm personal relationship with Lady Bedford known. The language of the two poems is guarded enough, but—if both refer to Lady Bedford—Donne may have felt extra precautions necessary in the case of the "Nocturnall" only.—Be that as it may, these two poems present Donne in a mood which is hardly to be matched by that of any orthodoxly "cynical" love poem of the canon. "Falling starre," for example, conveys a mood of pure elation, as compared with the black misery of these poems.

4

Farewell to love

Whilst yet to prove,
I thought there was some Deitie in love
So did I reverence, and gave
Worship; as Atheists at their dying houre
5    Call, what they cannot name, an unknowne power,
As ignorantly did I crave:
Thus when
Things not yet knowne are coveted by men,
Our desires give them fashion, and so
10   As they waxe lesser, fall, as they sise, grow.

But, from late faire
His highnesse sitting in a golden Chaire,
Is not lesse cared for after three dayes

By children, then the thing which lovers so
15    Blindly admire, and with such worship wooe;
        Being had, enjoying it decayes:
            And thence,
    What before pleas'd them all, takes but one sense,
      And that so lamely, as it leaves behinde
20    A kind of sorrowing dulnesse to the minde.

        Ah cannot wee,
    As well as Cocks and Lyons jocund be,
      After such pleasures? Unlesse wise
    Nature decreed (since each such Act, they say,
25    Diminisheth the length of life a day)
        This; as shee would man should despise
            The sport,
    Because that other curse of being short,
      And onely for a minute made to be
30    Eager, desires to raise posterity.

        Since so, my minde
    Shall not desire what no man else can finde,
      I'll no more dote and runne
    To pursue things which had indammag'd me.
35    And when I come where moving beauties be,
      As men doe when the summers Sunne
          Growes great,
    Though I admire their greatnesse, shun their heat;
      Each place can afford shadowes. If all faile,
40    'Tis but applying worme-seed to the Taile.

"Farewell to love," if it *is* orthodoxly "cynical," would be an exception to the statement above about a mood of deep depression. The poem expresses a strong reaction against physical love. This is not necessarily the reaction of an idealist revolted by the "grossness" of sex; it may as easily be the reaction of a hedonist disappointed because he misses the intensity of pleasure he desires. (For contemporary poems somewhat analogous in theme to Donne's, see Shakespeare's "Sonnet 129" and Ben Jonson's translation of a fragment of Petronius Arbiter.)

Superficially, the opening of the poem resembles that of "Aire and Angels." The speaker has a vague, unlocalized emotion of love. In this case, the worship turns out to be that of physical love, rather than that of a particular woman. Before we know the precise nature of the love, we are warned that the ideal may be shattered upon confrontation with the fact.

A piece of gilt gingerbread left over from a fair, is not so utterly ignored by children, after a day or so, as physical love is ignored on "Being had." All senses are pleased in anticipation of the event, but when it actually occurs, only the specifically-sexual sense is pleased—and that indifferently well—with the result that emotional depression ensues.

Since the precise meaning of the third stanza has cost explicators great pains to reveal it, and since their success has not been startling, I propose to save this stanza for last, as the major concern of the analysis—commenting here only that a certain dissatisfaction is expressed for the inadequacies of physical love, including its damaging effect on one's life-span. In the fourth stanza the speaker resolves to avoid this damaging effect. When he comes into the presence of beauties who incite his lust, he will admire their charms but shun their inflammatory qualities. One can usually reduce temptation to a minimum, but if worst comes to worst, there are always anaphrodisiacs.[5]

To return to the third stanza, commentators have had no difficulty in documenting the fact that cocks are traditionally lasivious, or that intercourse was believed to cut down one's life-span radically. But no one has proved, I think, that animals were supposed exempt from post-intercourse emotional depression, any more than they are exempt from the life-attrition of intercourse (cf. the Valentine epithalamium, line 7). The

saying has come down to us, "Post coitum omne animal triste."
Doctors disagree about the specific psychical implications of this
adage, but they would hardly limit its application to the human
being alone.[6] *All* (presumably male) animals are included—
not just the rational animal. I suspect an erotic pun in this
passage: the implications of *Cocks* are clear enough, and *Lyons*
must have borne superficial phonetic resemblance to *loins*
['lɔɪənz] for the former; [lɔɪnz] for the latter).[7] Why can't
*we*—the argument runs—why can't *we* (the whole personality,
the complex of the senses) experience pleasure just as well as
genitals and loins ("one sense") do?—The question is meant
to be rhetorical, but a possible answer occurs to the speaker.
Before we paraphrase this answer, we might well ask why
Donne fails to use the forthright phrase *Cocks and Loins*. This
poem is not particularly inclined towards euphemism: a more
adequate reason is needed. I believe that, at face value, Donne's
phrase is intended to evoke the nostalgic thought that animals,
like infants, are exempt from ethical responsibility (cf. "Holy
Sonnet IX" ["If poysonous mineralls . . ."]). Why *shouldn't*
we enjoy ourselves all day, as animals (supposedly) do?—I will
not insist on the presence of a pun here, but the reader is justly
suspicious (I think) of the unusual juxtaposition of cocks and
lions, with reference to lust, and of the apparent assumption
that animals are immune to post-coital emotional depression.

In lines 16-20, the second stanza cites two related curses
pertaining to physical love. The first mentioned is that of disappointment in the act itself; the other is that of post-coital
emotional depression. The third stanza deals with the implications of these curses—the two curses here being taken in re-
verse order. To follow the original order, the curse of inadequacy
aims at the raising of posterity; that is, man's brevity of vitality
reminds him of the transitory nature of life, and he engages in
intercourse to insure continuity by procreation. Nature's major

purpose, the preservation of the race, is consequently served. But intercourse results in gradual attrition of life, each act subtracting a day. Nature's secondary purpose is that of lengthening the life of the current generation; hence the second curse: the emotional reaction operates as a check which partially discourages intercourse. Nature supplies, as a resultant for these components of forces, the minimum amount of intercourse required for maximum chances of propagation.

By Donne's deliberate design, the emotional implications of this stanza are working at cross-purposes with the conceptual implications. That fact is what causes the difficulty in explication. The speaker ironically pretends to be grateful for the thought fulness of "wise/Nature"; actually, he regards nature's expedient as a curse. Disappointment in the act itself is also a curse, but the attrition of the act—which ultimately causes all the trouble—is exempt from imprecations: it has no immediate effect on the pleasure of intercourse. The criterion is hedonistic: In what ways are my pleasures circumscribed, in intercourse?— The obliquity of this hedonistic attitude is matched by that which appears (at least) to be in the *Cocks and Lyons* phrase we have examined.

In the light of the stanza's general implications, ambiguity appears in the clause *as shee would man should despise/The sport*. In one sense it means *as if nature wanted man to despise intercourse;* i. e., nature *does not* want such, since intercourse is necessary for preservation of the race. The second sense gives us nature's precise attitude: *because nature wants man to despise the sport as sport*. There is a contrast between enjoying oneself, and raising posterity; if a man embraces intercourse for pleasure, he will propagate the race, but he will also burn himself out in no time.

The sense of dissatisfaction with sex is expressed most forcibly in lines 28-30. Conceptually, as we have noted, the curse "of being short,/And onely for a minute made to be/ Eager," refers to the transitory nature of life in general and mature vitality in particular. Emotionally, this curse refers to the shortcomings of the sexual instrument—including the briefness of sexual vigor. (Were it not for man's resulting insight into mortality, the inadequacies of the act would check excessive intercourse. without the aid of the depressing postlude.) The precise physical implications of the curse are made evident, I think, by a cross-reference to "Loves Alchymie," which also expresses disappointment with physical love ("lovers dreame a rich and long delight,/But get a winter-seeming summers night"). There is a bit of snobbishness in the speaker's question, "Ends love in this, that my man,/Can be as happy'as I can; If he can/Endure the short scorne of a Bridegroomes play?" (Ll. 15-17.) The reference to happiness is ironic. (Otherwise, there is a close parallel in the Lord and Lady Witherspoon joke whose punch-line runs: "You'll simply have to stop it; it's too good for them.") *Short scorne* has at least two implications: 1. the bride scorns the shortness of the bridegroom's organ (though her scorn may be short-lived); 2. intercourse results in rapid "de-horning" (see the *NED*'s etymology for *scorn*, regarding possible Italian influence on the word in the 16 and 17 c.).[8]— Both these implications of shortness combine in "Farewell to love," I think, with the additional implications of human mortality. The note on which the poem ends it not one of *carpe diem*. Instead of indulging himself during the brief years left to him, the speaker resolves to forego physical love—not to lengthen life at the expense of his own pleasure, but to avoid the disappointment which intercourse inevitably brings. He is a hedonist in a world where *carpe diem* is impossible.

5

From the analysis of a poem on sex, we proceed to a discussion of the problem of sex and high seriousness.—C. S. Lewis is an unusually sound scholar and sane critic—and he is well aware of the dangers involved in what he calls the "Personal Heresy."[9] One mark of this heresy is the entangling of an author's biography with his works. Consequently, when Lewis tells us that Donne's secular-love poems are based on "a medieval sense of the sinfulness of sexuality,"[10] we are inclined to give his statement considerable attention. Miss Joan Bennett has offered a refutation of Lewis's thesis,[11] but the argument of her essay is not altogether convincing.

Donne's more explicit comment on the problems of sex occurs after his taking of Orders. If he then had the attitude Lewis mentions, he may have had the same attitude earlier, since this "medieval sense" is traceable back to the Church Fathers, whom Donne probably first read in his early youth as the member of a Roman Catholic family. George R. Potter tells us that this attitude is expressed frequently in Donne's sermons. Here is Potter's note to one passage: "Donne's lifelong preoccupation with the sexual processes appears frequently in his sermons, with this emphasis on their sinfulness—an attitude which reflects that of St. Augustine (that the begetting of children is not sinful, but passionate and uncontrollable delight in the act is) but which is not to modern readers as persuasive as his earlier justification of sexual desire, in *The Ecstasy*."[12]

Potter chooses his words carefully here, with reference to Dr. Donne (whatever we may think of his characterization of "The Extasie"), but the passage annotated is such that the note may give us a slightly erroneous impression.—Here is the passage in Donne's sermon:

The rising and setting of the sun, height of prosperity and depth of adversity, we observe, but we observe not the degrees of the ascending of this sun, how God hath led us every step and preserved us in many particular dangers in our rising, nor the degrees of the descending of this sun we observe not, we observe not that God would show us in the loss of our children, the sinful wantonness in which they were begotten and conceived, in the loss of our health, the sinful voluptuousness in which it was pampered, in the loss of goods, the sinful extortion in which they were gathered....[13]

Potter's note prevents us from assuming that Donne regarded the act of begetting children as necessarily sinful, but the passage in Donne may leave us with the impression that *in practice* the act of begetting is characteristically sinful. Now Donne, in another sermon, cautions his hearers against assuming that sudden death is necessarily God's punishment for sin.[14] There is no discrepancy between the two passages: in cases of personal calamity, we should judge others charitably, giving them the benefit of the doubt, but we should examine our own consciences with great care; perhaps a specific sin of ours has brought the calamity on.—At any rate, the first passage cannot be cited as evidence that the sexual act—in Donne's view—is necessarily sinful.

There is another passage which, taken out of its context in the Sermons, might seem to claim that the act is indeed sinful by its own nature—even when begetting is involved. Donne is illustrating the swiftness with which human captivity to sin comes upon us. " . . . In the generation of our parents, we were conceived in sin; this is, they sinned in that action; so we were conceived in sin; in their sin. And in ourselves, we were submitted to sin, in that very act of generation, because then we became in part the subject of original sin."[15] Donne's position seems to be even more rigorous than that of St. Augustine, but in the light of statements elsewhere in the Sermons, we can say that Donne is merely lending emphasis to his point—or perhaps borrowing emphasis illegitimately. Original sin *is* transmitted by the act of generation; sinful behavior *may or may not be* involved in this act.

Elsewhere Donne tells his hearers to enter into their bedside prayers "with a repentant consideration; that in that bed
thy children were conceived in sin, that in that bed thou hast
turned marriage which God afforded thee for remedy, and
physic, to voluptuousness, and licentiousness; that thou hast
made that bed which God gave thee for rest, and for reparation
of thy weary body, to be as thy dwelling, and delight, and the
bed of idleness, and stupidity."[16] Obviously, not everyone
abuses his bed by idleness, and not everyone abuses it
by turning marriage into licentiousness (whether or not
this licentiousness involves conceiving children in sin apart
from original sin). Donne's message is directed to whom it may
concern—not, of course, that everyone may not take "repentant
consideration" of *some* sin he has committed; the prayers occur
at the bedside, and Donne chooses, for illustration, sins peculiar to the bed.

Donne refers repeatedly to three uses of marriage. Here is
one significant passage in this connection:

. . . God hath given man a wife, *ad adjutorium, ad sobolem,
ad medicinam;* for a help, for children, and for a remedy, and
physic. Now for the first, society, and increase, we love naturally; we would not be banished, we would not be robbed, we
would not be alone, we would not be poor; society and increase,
every man loves; but doth any man love physic? he takes it for
necessity; but does he love it? Husbands therefore are to love
wives *ad sobolem,* as the mothers of their children; *ad adjutorium,* as the comforters of their lives; but for that, which is *ad
medicinam,* for physic, to avoid burning, to avoid fornication,
that is not the subject of our love, our love is not to be placed
upon that; for so it is a love, *quia mulier,* because she is a woman,
and not *quia uxor,* because she is my wife. A man may be a
drunkard at home, with his own wine. and never go out to tav-
erns; a man may be an adulterer in his wife's bosom, though he
seek not strange women.[17]

Elsewhere, Donne has noted that, although marriage is intended

other adjustment involves the possibility that Donne's attitude was considerably less rigorous before he felt the need of preaching to himself (as Walton said his habit was, in the pulpit); Dr. Donne unquestionably experienced a strong reaction against the slightest appearance of evil in his former life.—I suspect that the two adjustments would cancel one another out, more or less effectively. Donne's view, then—with some liberalization —would approximate that expressed in "The Extasie": that our bodies are not "drosse to us, but allay." From the standpoint of the naked spirit, they *are* dross, but we must reckon on their existence, whether we will or no. Our bodies are the alloy which enables us—while living on earth—to communicate with one another, and they are the allaying influence which quells the concupiscence the flesh is heir to. Even as a priest in the Church of England, Donne inclines toward the Catholic tradition, not identifying it exclusively with the Roman Church.

Assuming that Jack Donne acted on (by reacting against) such a view of sex, can we point out ways in which the secular-love poems demonstrate such a background of belief? C. S. Lewis has not convinced me, I am afraid, that the poems are actually informed with "a medieval sense of the sinfulness of sexuality"—or even, for the most part, with a heightened sense of potential sinfulness in sex. It seems to me that the general run of the poems are informed with a cheerful amoralism. But, even if Lewis is wrong on this score, he may be justified in citing Donne's personal attitude towards sex.—We have already noted that the secular-love poems are basically dramatic in structure; that fact, of course, hardly exempts the poet from some sort of stand on moral issues. We scarcely need a psychoanalyst to tell us that Donne was preoccupied with sex, but we are at a loss for an attitude which can reconcile cheerfully amoral poems with Platonic or Petrarchan poems on the one hand, and crudely cynical poems on the other.

The sexual melancholy expressed in "Farewell to love" has, as we have noted, no necessary relationship with spiritual misgivings. Nor is there necessarily a valid comment in "The Calme," with its reference to "the queasie paine/Of being belov'd, and loving" (ll. 40f.). "Farewell to love" and the passage from "The Calme" may express merely a libertine impatience at the thwarting of full hedonism. The hedonist wants what he wants when he wants it—not at other times, when a woman's love obligates him, or an ugly woman wooes him. He is similarly annoyed when his advances are not welcomed, or when his mistress breaks faith with him before he is ready to break faith with her.

That Jack Donne was a hedonist has been called in questtion by Allen R. Benham, in an article called "The Myth of John Donne the Rake."[26] I am not at all sure that the article succeeds in exploding the "myth." At any rate, the whole question is one worth examining. The name of St. Augustine comes to our attention at once, in this connection. Of all the patristic writers, St. Augustine seems to have been Donne's favorite—and that not merely on theological grounds. Looking back over the pattern of his own life, Donne evidently noted a similarity to the pattern of St. Augustine's life. In each case. a very worldly man of learning had unexpectedly become a man of God.

In his youth, Augustine had not only committed carnal sins, but had invented more for public recountal, lest he seem backward in profligacy among his contemporaries. In one of his sermons, Donne quotes St. Augustine on this matter ,supplying his own translation of the Latin. We might note that the Latin passages which Donne translates for his congregation, are often rather freely paraphrased in Donne's version. In this case, however, the translation of St. Augustine is unusually odd, and hence may reveal something about Jack Donne's own approach to poetry: "*Audiebam eos exaltantes flagitia,* sayes that tender blessed Father, I saw it was thought wit, to make Sonnets of their own sins, *Et libebat facere, non libidine facti, sed libidine laudis,* I sinn'd, not for the pleasure I had in the sin, but for the pride that I had to write feelingly of it."[27] If this is indeed a description of Jack Donne's verse technique, it may help to explain the frequency of dramatic structure in the early poems, which—even if they are based on immediate personal experience —represent independent psychological situations. In this connection, there is an interesting statement in the prose letter to Sir Robert Ker which prefaces "An hymne to the Saints, and to Marquesse Hamylton"; the body of the letter is pertinent here, as the setting for the statement:

> I Presume you rather try what you can doe in me, then what I can doe in verse; you know my uttermost when it was best, and even then I did best when I had least truth for my subjects. In this present case there is so much truth as it defeats all Poetry. Call therefore this paper by what name you will, and, if it bee not worthy of him, nor of you, nor of mee, smother it, and bee that the sacrifice. If you had commanded mee to have waited on his body to Scotland and preached there, I would have embraced the obligation with more alacrity; But, I thanke you that you would command me that which I was loath to doe, for, even that hath given a tincture of merit to the obedience of [etc.]. . . .

The precise values of *my uttermost, best,* and *truth* are in question here. It seems likely to me that these words refer to Donne's early dramatic monologues, with *truth* signifying both *biographical or autobiographical fact* and *didactic intent* (*propagation of the eternal verities*). Donne evidently feels that this elegy is inferior, from the standpoint of literary merit, because in it he is working too close to biographical fact and didactic purpose, but too far away from inspiration.

As moralist rather than literary critic, Dr. Donne was explicit in condemning the sort of wit Jack Donne had indulged in. "Scurrile and obscene language; yea, mis-interpretable words, such as may bear an ill sense,"[28] are capable of compromising purity of heart. Dr. Donne (or the editorial *I* of his sermons) even finds it easy to read obscene meanings into his own prayers;[29] he has presumably been betrayed by habit—by what he calls elsewhere "concupiscence of witt."[30] On occasion he may have been "mov'd to seeme religious/Only to vent wit."[31] Dr. Donne would make a clean break with "Fame, Wit, Hopes," the false mistresses of his youth.[32]

Donne's renunciation of the harmful effects of wit, is well illustrated by a passage in which Dr. Donne virtually preaches at the sins of Jack Donne. In his *Paradoxes and Problemes* Donne had dwelt on the question, "Why Hath the Common Opinion Afforded Women Soules?" Of course women have souls, says Dr. Donne; any contrary belief or pretense at belief is mere "petulancy and wantonness of wit, and . . . extravagancy of paradoxes."[33]—But the later Donne never lost his sense of perspective, insofar as the distinction between life and art was concerned. Speaking of Roman Catholic women who (he claims) prostitute themselves to gain converts, Donne notes that this practice "is somewhat a strange Topique, to draw arguments of religion from."[34] Yet as a poet he finds no sacrilege in the imaginative representation of much the same effect: the association of sexual promiscuity with the Christian religion. Christ is the only delighted cuckold; as we have noted in Chapter 5, above, "Holy Sonnet XVIII" ends with the paradox that Christ's spouse "is most true, and pleasing to [him], then/ When she'is embrac'd and open to most men."

Donne is condensing a great deal into small compass, I think, when he characterizes fame, wit, and hopes as the false mistresses of his youth. Donne pinned his hopes on fame and wit, that is; betrayal came as a matter of course. I doubt that the desire for fame had much to do with literary fame, except insofar as a reputation for wit and sophistication would advance his worldly career. It may not have been worldly ambition which caused Donne to reject the unpopular Catholicism in which he had been reared, but his renunciation of a Christian moral code indicates that he was willing to accept the standards of the courtiers with whom he was competing for fame. Donne probably, like Augustine, committed and advertised carnal sins in his youth—partly because the flesh offered a real temptation, and partly because it was fashionable to be debauched. Unlike Augustine, Donne seems to have taken pride in writing "feelingly" of the sin—in constructing a dramatic situation from which Donne the person was somehow abstracted, though the basic material was that of personal experience. There would seem to be some truth in that favorite assumption of modern critics: that Donne is primarily interested in representing psychological traits.

I have tried to indicate that Donne could not claim the exemptions of neutrality, merely by adopting the dramatic mode. It is up to us to find, if it exists, a central tendency which runs through the early poems, accounting for their divergencies of approach, and also tying them up with the poems of the later period. The attitude of cynical sophistication will hardly meet the requirements, though this attitude is presented at arm's length, in the dramatic mode. To a greater extent than the "cynical" poems—and to at least as great an extent, I think, as the Petrarchan or Platonic poems—"The Extasie" approximates the position which Dr. Donne would accept toward matters of secular love. But even "The Extasie" is not central in the manner which I would mention here. The central poems, I think, are those which characterize lovers as private worlds.

### 6

As a study, the economy of images has interesting possibilities. Such a study would not involve, like Rugoff's, the mechanical classification of images under the heading of their sources in the trades, professions, etc. Nor would it merely point out the fact that, despite the wide area from which images are drawn in Donne, we find certain images repeated again and again—as if Donne were forced to practice economy. On repeated occasions, a particular incident tended to call up in Donne's consciousness a partciular illustration from a different field. For example, whenever a quiet, unobtrusive action became the subject of discussion, Donne was almost invariably reminded of a virtuous man meeting death calmly.—But economy of images, as I envision the study, would attempt to show the significance of patterns in repetition (with the understanding that all repetitions need not be highly significant). (Rugoff deals with significances, of course, but primarily in terms external to the poems.)

If we may coin a portmanteau word, after the fashion of James Joyce, the matter becomes one of the *iconomy* of images— the manner in which reiterated images constitute icons or symbols (and the number of such symbols is relatively small in Donne). Any study—along Freudian lines—of Donne's erotic imagery, is likely to take this form. At least one such study has been made;[35] the results are fantastically unconvincing, but the basic theory may not be itself at fault.— The icon I choose to investigate as central, may—but need not— be interpreted in Freudian terms. It is simply the image of lovers as private worlds. Altogether, Donne uses the microcosm theme in both verse and prose, to secure a number of different (though related) effects, but the use of the theme in the love poems is both uniform and striking. If we were not already aware of the dangers involved in speculating on the symbolic significance of this recurrent theme, we would have only to turn to William Empson's fantastic conjectures in this connection (Empson, however, is concerned with the microcosm complex, only to the extent that it fits in with Logos implications like those in the *Anniversaries*).[36] We proceed in this matter with some reservations about the revelatory powers of imagery.

In Freudian terms, the miscrocosm icon represents, I think, a sort of womb-regression. In the actual world, love lacked precisely that tidiness and coziness which the private world supplied. In "The good-morrow," the lovers' souls "watch not one another out of feare"; treachery is out of the question. "Who is so safe as we?" the speaker of "The Anniversary" asks. " . . . None can doe/Treason to us, except one of us two./True and false fears let us refraine. . . ." The question of fidelity is no longer a source of anxiety.

The modest ambition of Donne's lovers to withdraw into their private world, is contrasted repeatedly with secular ambition. "Let sea-discoverers to new worlds have gone,/. . . Let us possesse one world [a world in common; a single world, as opposed to a multiplicity]. . . ."[37] " . . . Take you a course, get you a place,/. . . What you will, approve/So you will let me love."[38] "Me which hath businesse, and makes love, doth doe/ Such wrong, as when a maryed man doth wooe."[39]—This last quotation ostensibly refers to the Christian moral code; actually, the married man's wrong is not his infidelity to wife and family, but his treatment of the paramour as a sometime thing.

Renunciation of worldly values is a mark of religious conviction. In "The Canonization," the linking of the microcosm with the private religion of love, is hardly accidental. Here the lovers gladly forego secular ambition; they have withdrawn from the world and become "one anothers hermitage." The question of Christian morality never enters the poem at all. The lovers may or may not be married; at any rate, they have not renounced the full enjoyment of sexual love. Here there is no sense even of the potential sinfulness of sexuality, but there *is* a deep dissatisfaction with the "rage" and restless ambition of the world.

Together the lovers constitute a phoenix, but they also constitute, in the terms of another poem, "Two Phoenixes, whose joyned breasts/Are unto one another mutuall nests."[40] Their love combines the cloister and the hearth.

### 7

The two great themes of Donne are love and death. It has not been sufficiently demonstrated, I think, that love (as romantic love) and death (as literal loss of life) have virtually no significant interrelationships in Donne. The mind of Dr. Donne was obsessed with intimations of mortality, and of the immortality which divine love could provide. For him, romantic love took a distinctly subordinate position: it is virtually absent from the Sermons, and present in the Divine Poems only as the index to a higher type of love.

Again, death is constantly making its appearance in metaphorical form, in the poems of secular love. Absence is death; intercourse is death; the beloved's scorn is death. But we never find in Donne, as we do in Marvell, a macabre combination of the themes of love and death, with a morbid dwelling on the activities of worms, and a linking of sex-attrition with *carpe diem*. In the sermons of Donne the worms are present in force, but it is easy to overestimate the importance of the macabre in the secular-love poems. Donne devotes a great deal of attention to wills, funerals, graves, corpses, etc.—but mainly because of their non-macabre imaginative potentialities. Unlike Webster, he did not—as a poet of romantic love—see the skull beneath the skin. The famous reference in "The Will" to the inutility of "a Sun diall in a grave," has undeniable imaginative power, yet—in the conceptual structure of the poem—it is an exact parallel to the less evocative "gold in Mines, where none doth draw it forth." Both comparisons involve a buried location (and hence have potentially macabre implications), but these comparisons simply fit in with the basic assumption of the poem:

that the speaker is dying, and not dying in vain. His "death," that is, is merely a device which clusters around it, on a logical basis, disparaging remarks about love and the beloved.—Even the famous wreath of hair in "The Funerall" and "The Relique," is somewhat less grotesque than it has been represented as being, I think. Eliot is altogether justified in praising the associations in the line, "A bracelet of bright haire about the bone," but this is not necessarily a macabre—albiet a genuine—Metaphysical effect. We have noted a somewhat similar effect in "Elegie XVI," where actual physical death and romantic love focus, as themes, on the visual image of the white Alps; but the juxtaposition of the two themes is hardly typical of Donne's poems.

There is undoubtedly continuity between Jack Donne and Dr. Donne, but we have gone too far—I think—in our reaction against the oversimplification which cut Donne in two. The macabre sense of mortality, and the strong sense of the potential sinfulness of sexuality—these are undoubtedly present in Dr. Donne, and perhaps they lie dormant in Jack Donne, but they seldom get into the early poems in any effective way, and they are less than characteristic of the later poems.

There are marked similarities in method, however, between the priest's explication of a sermon text, and the poet's development of a theme. We are impressed in both cases with the way in which Donne wrings every possible implication out of his material. Only a Donne idolator would claim success for him in every instance. The question is not whether his effects are farfetched: they *are,* almost invariably, for such is the technique. The question is whether, after all, they are worth the carriage.—This resurrection of a dead metaphor is not mine, but Dr. Johnson's. As a critic of the Metaphysicals, he is unsympathetic but fair. In playing the Devil's Advocate for them, on this occasion, he is virtually using their own technique: " . . . If their conceits were far-fetched, they were often worth the carriage. To write on their plan it was at least necessary to read and think."[41]

### 8

I maintain that Jack Donne was a disillusioned idealist. If the characterization is to mean anything, I must define its limits of applicability. Every cynic, of course, is a disillusioned idealist, but there is surely a valid distinction between the cynic embittered by the restrictions life places on the selfish pleasures he can enjoy, and the cynic embittered by a time which is out of joint. I suspect that Donne was both of these cynics, for a time, but even in "Farewell to love" (as viewed in the context of the other early poems), there is implicit dissatisfaction with the theory as well as the practice of hedonism. The Platonic and Petrarchan poems represent a reaction, but no solution: it is hard to convince oneself that the problems of sex do not exist.

The term *animal spirits* (in the modern sense) can explain a great deal about the mind of Jack Donne, I think. Animal spirits betrayed him into temptations of the flesh, and animal spirits guarded him (for the most part) from bitterness and a profound sense of depression at the transitory nature of human love (and at the rigorous Catholic view of sexual pleasure). As we have noted, the prevailing tone of the early poems is one of cheerful amoralism, and it is hard to believe that Donne hated every minute of it. "Womans constancy," after a diatribe against feminine fickleness, frankly admits to equal fickleness on the part of the male speaker; Donne may actually have owned this mood.—But Jack Donne's celebration of variety in love, is essentially a forced effort to make a virtue of a necessity. In addition to enduring the disappointments of physical love, one must be prepared to suffer "the queasie paine/Of being belov'd, and loving"—of never quite bringing the lover and the beloved into rapport.

As Mr. Cleanth Brooks has noted, "Donne's imagination

seems obsessed with the problem of unity; the sense in which the lovers become one—the sense in which the soul is united with God."[42] Part of the problem of unity involves the relationship of soul to body in the human being. Donne's preoccupation with this relationship survived his willingness to exalt physical love. In "The Litanie" Donne begs, "From thinking us all soule, neglecting thus/Our mutuall duties, Lord deliver us" (ll. 143f.). Whether or not the reference is to the marital debt, the body's claim to recognition of rights is being advanced.

But recognition of the body's claim is made most frequently —at this stage—in terms of imagery proper, with reference to the relatedness of things. Secular love is cited in imagery pertaining to sacred themes. As a Metaphysical poet, Donne is committed (by popular definition) to demonstrating this type and other types of the relatedness of things. For this purpose he utilizes the pun, as well as the figure of speech. Christ himself used a normative pun in changing Simon's name to Peter, a rock; as we have noted, Dr. Donne never hesitates to use the pun in his sermons and sacred poems. By the use of the pun and the extended metaphor (among other effects), Donne was able to achieve that fusion of emotion and intellection for which he is currently famous.

Above all, Donne never fails to utilize a potential relationship between the microcosm and the macrocosm. In terms of books, "Man is an abridgment of all the world. . . ."[43] In terms of cosmic structure, he is "a little world made cunningly/Of Elements, and an Angelike spright. . . ."[44] In terms of circles and compasses, we may find a prose variant of the famous figure in the Mourning valediction:

. . . [The martyrs'] death was a birth to them into another life, into the glory of God; it ended one circle, and created another; for immortality, and eternity is a circle too; not a circle where two points meet, but a circle made at once; this life is a circle, made with a compass, that passes from point to point; that life is a circle stamped with a print, an endless, and perfect circle, as soon as it begins. Of this circle, the mathematician is our great and good God; the other circle we make up ourselves; we bring the cradle, and grave together by a course of nature.[45]

The progress from dust to dust is superseded by instant eternity.

From Donne, Ernest Hemingway borrowed the title of his novel on the Spanish Civil War. In Donne's name, we may presume to borrow it back, as combined with the title of another Hemingway novel. We can imagine Donne's lover advising his lady: Never send to know for whom the sun rises; it rises for us.—The lovers constitute a private solar system, with the sun rising and setting at their behest. "Shine here to us," Donne's speaker says, addressing the rising sun, "and thou art every where;/This bed thy center[of revolution] is, these walls, thy spheare [periphery of revolution]." Divine love hardly seemed accessible to the Donne of the early period—any more than, in the "rage" of the secular world, constant love seemed possible between woman and man. But the microcosm symbol of security in love, prefigured Donne's attachment to the source of genuine spiritual strength. The pattern was still provided by secular love: " . . . God having . . . married soul and body in one man, and man and God, in one Christ, he marries this Christ to the church."[46]

# Notes

## Chapter 1

### An Invocation to the Donne Canon

1. Quoted in J. B. Leishman, *The Metaphysical Poets*: *Donne, Herbert, Vaughan, Traherne* (Oxford, 1934), p. 39.
2. See James Thurber, *Let Your Mind Alone! and Other More or Less Inspirational Pieces* (New York, 1937), pp. 75 f.
3. See Hugh I'Anson Fausset, *John Donne*: *A Study in Discord* (London, 1924).
4. See Rosemary Freeman, *English Emblem Books* (London, 1948), pp. 146 f.; see also Josef Lederer, "John Donne and the Emblematic Practice," *RES*, XXII (1946), 182-200.
5. See John Crowe Ransom, *The New Criticism* (Norfolk, Conn.; 1941), p. 190.
6. See Milton A. Rugoff, *Donne's Imagery*: *A Study in Creative Sources* (New York, 1939), and Caroline Spurgeon, *Shakespeare's Imagery and What It Tells Us* (Cambridge, 1935).
7. See Rosemond Tuve, *Elizabethan and Metaphysical Imagery*: *Renaissance Poetic and Twentieth-Century Critics* (Chicago, 1947).
8. René Wellek, "The Concept of Baroque in Literary Scholarship," *Journal of Aesthetics and Art Criticism*, V (1946), 77-109; p. 90. A note attributes the Johnson quotation to " 'Life of Abraham Cowley' in *Lives of the English Poets.*"
9. René Wellek and Austin Warren, *Theory of Literature* (New York, 1949), pp. 214f.; the chapter on imagery is by Mr. Warren
10. T. S. Eliot, "John Donne," *The Nation* & *the Athenaeum*, XXXIII (1923), 331 f.; p. 332.
11. Quoted in H. W. Garrod, ed., *John Donne*: *Poetry and Prose* (Oxford, 1946), p. i (small Roman numeral).
12. See *die* in Eric Partridge, *Shakespeare's Bawdy*: *A Literary* & *Psychological Essay and a Comprehensive Glossary* (New York, 1948).
13. See Don Cameron Allen, "John Donne's Knowledge of Ren-

aissance Medicine," *JEGP*, XLII (1943), 322-342; p. 332.

14. See Allen Tate, *Reason in Madness*: *Critical Essays* (New York, 1941), pp. 90 f.

15. See Helge Kökeritz, "Shakespeare's Pronounciation," *Moderna Språk*, XLIII (1949), 149-168; pp. 155 and 162.

16. See Pierre Legouis, *Donne the Craftsman*: *An Essay Upon the Structure of the Songs and Sonets* (Paris, 1928), pp. 61-71.

17. See *glass of virginity* in Partridge, *op. cit.*

18. See Kökeritz, *loc. cit.*, p. 161.

19. See John Crowe Ransom, "Honey and Gall," *Southern Review*, VI (1940), 2-19; p. 10. Cf. Ransom, *op. cit.*, p. 185.

20. See W. B. Yeats, *Essays*, Revised Edition (New York, 1924), p. 492.

21. See *Ben Jonson's Conversations with William Drummond of Hawthornden*, ed. R. F. Patterson (London, 1923), p. 5; cf. Garrod, *op. cit.*, p. 80.

22. Jonson, *op. cit.*, p.5.

23. See I. A. Richards, *The Philosophy of Rhetoric* (New York, 1936), pp. 96 ff.

24. Rugoff, *op. cit.*, p. 144.

25. Charles E. Merrill, ed., Donne's *Letters to Severall Persons of Honour* (New York, 1910), p. 44.

26. See Charles M. Coffin, *John Donne and the New Philosophy* (New York, 1937).

27. Jonson, *op. cit.*, pp. 12 and 18.

28. See John Hayward, ed., *John Donne . . .*: *Complete Poetry and Selected Prose* (London, 1930), p. 751.

29. *Ibid.*, p. 744.

30. See Logan Pearsall Smith, *Donne's Sermons*: *Selected Passages with an Essay* (Oxford, 1919), p. 53.

31. Hayward, *op. cit.*, p. 746.

32. See Cleanth Brooks, *Modern Poetry and the Tradition* (Chapel Hill, 1939), p. 27.

## Chapter 2

### Patterns of Parting

1. See T. S. Eliot, *Selected Essays*: 1917-1932 (New York, 1932), pp. 242 f.

2. Hayward, *op. cit.*, p. 755.

3. *Ibid.*, p. 759.

4. *Ibid.*, p. 730.

5. *Ibid.*, p. 727.

6. See Francis Thompson, *Shelley* (New York, 1909), pp. 50-53.

7. See William Empson, *Seven Types of Ambiguity*, Second Edition (New York, 1947), pp. 139-145.

8. Henry Alford, ed., *The Works of John Donne* . . ., 6 vol. (London, 1839); I, 268 f.

9. See Allen, *loc. cit.*, p. 332.

10. See Garrod, *op. cit.*, p. 110.

11. See Coffin, *op. cit.*, pp. 98-100.

12. See Donald A. Stauffer, *The Nature of Poetry* (New York, 1946), p. 279.

13. See Kökeritz, *loc. cit.*, pp. 159 and 161.

14. Hayward, *op. cit.*, p. 690.

## Chapter 3

### *Off With That Girdle!*

1. George Williamson, review of Rugoff, *MLN*, LVI (1941), 626-628; p. 627.

2. *Works of Robert Herrick*, ed. A. W. Pollard, 2 vol., Revised Edition (London, 1898); I, 229.

3. Eliot, *op. cit.*, p. 246.

4. *Ibid.*, p. 247.

5. Eliot, *loc. cit.*, p. 332.

6. S. L. Bethell, "Two Streams from Helicon," Part III, *The New English Weekly*, XXVIII (1945-46), 213f.; p. 214.

7. See Sigmund Freud, *A General Introduction to Psycho-Analysis*, trans. Joan Riviere (New York, 1935), p. 139.

8. See *coun* in Partridge, *op. cit.*

9. See Laurence Sterne, *Tristram Shandy*, ed. James A. Work (New York, 1940), p. 510.

10. See *come* in Partridge, *op. cit.*

11. See Allen, *loc. cit.*, p. 339 .

12. Don Cameron Allen, "Donne's Phoenix," *MLN*, LXII (1947), 340-342; p. 341.

13. *Ibid.*, p. 342.

# Notes

## Chapter 4

### The Poet as Lawyer

1. See Williamson, *loc. cit.*, p. 627.
2. John Dryden, *The Critical and Miscellaneous Prose Works . . .*, ed. Edmond Malone, 3 vol. (London, 1800); III, 79.
3. See Allen, ". . . Renaissance Medicine," p. 334.
4. See Legouis, *op. cit.*, pp. 61-71.
5. See, for example, Frank A. Doggett, "Donne's Platonism," *Sewanee Review,* XLII (1934), 274-92; Merritt Y. Hughes, "Kidnapping Donne," pp. 61-89 in *Essays in Criticism, Second Series (University of California Publications in English,* IV; Berkeley, 1934), and "The Lineage of 'The Extasie,' " *MLR,* XXVII (1932), 1-5; and George R. Potter, "Donne's *Extasie,* Contra Legouis," *PQ,* XV (1936), 247-253.
6. Gretchen L. Finney, "Ecstasy and Music in Seventeenth-Century England," *JHI,* VIII (1947), 153-186; p. 178.
7. William Empson, *Some Versions of Pastoral* (London, 1935), pp. 133 f.
8. My comments are based on Empson's classroom lectures, Kenyon School of English, 1948.
9. Alford, IV, 485.
10. See George Williamson, "Textual Difficulties in the Interpretation of Donne's Poetry," *MP,* XXXVIII (1940), 37-72; p. 57.
11. Alford, IV, 368.
12. *Ibid.,* IV, 74.
13. *Ibid.,* I, 362.
14. See Wellek and Warren, *op. cit.,* pp. 180 f.
15. Alford, IV, 367.
16. See Richard Jordan, *Handbuch der Mittelenglischen Grammatik,* Part 1, Second Edition (Heidelberg, 1934), pp. 150 f.; see also H. C. Wyld, *A History of Modern Colloquial English,* Third Edition (Oxford, 1936), pp. 298-300.
17. See George Williamson, "Textual Difficulties in . . . Donne's Poetry," pp. 38 f.

## Chapter 5

### In Sonnets Pretty Romes

1. *The Works of Samuel Johnson . . .,* ed. Arthur Murphy, 12 vol.

(London, 1801); IX, 63 f.

2. Smith, *op. cit.*, pp. 25 f.

3. Williamson, "Textual Difficulties in . . . Donne's Poetry," pp. 42-45.
   (1942), 257-285; pp. 269-271.

4. Ralph Waldo Emerson, *Poems* (London, 1914), p. 6 ("The Sphinx").

5. See Cleanth Brooks, *The Well Wrought Urn*: *Studies in the Structure of Poetry* (New York, 1947), pp. 10-17.

6. See Edgar H. Duncan, "Donne's Alchemical Figures," *ELH*, IX

7. For a clearcut use of *canonize* with reference to poems, see Merrill, *op. cit.*, p. 29.

8. Brooks, *Urn*, pp. 12 f.

9. Empson, *Ambiguity*, pp. 145 f.

10. Hayward, *op. cit.*, p. 759.

11. Bethell, *loc. cit.*, p. 213.

12. Merrill, *op. cit.*, pp. 25 f.

13. See Williamson, review of Rugoff, p. 628.

14. See Leah Jonas, *The Divine Science*: *The Aesthetic of Some Representative Seventeenth-Century English Poets* (New York, 1940), p. 201.

15. See *Modern Poetry*, pp. 24 f.

16. *Idem.*

17. *Idem.*

18. Quoted in Evelyn M. Simpson, *A Study of the Prose Works of John Donne*, Second Edition (Oxford, 1948), p. 313. I have spelled out typographically-troublesome abbreviations, and inserted (within brackets) conjectural punctuation, etc.

19. Garrod, *op. cit.*, p. 79.

20. *Ibid.*, p. 81.

21. See H. M. Paull, *Literary Ethics*: *A Study in the Growth of the Literary Conscience* (New York, 1929), p. 328.

22. See Allen R. Benham, "The Myth of John Donne the Rake," pp. 273-281 in *Renaissance Studies in Honor of Hardin Craig*, ed. Baldwin Maxwell, *et al.* (Stanford, 1941); p. 279.

23. Jonson, *op. cit.*, p. 5.

24. *Ibid.*, p. 12.

25. *Ibid.*, p. 18.

26. *Ibid.*, p. 8.

# Notes

27. *Ibid.*, p. 36.
28. C. H. Herford, and Percy and Evelyn Simpson, ed., *Ben Jonson*, 8 vol. (Oxford, 1925-47); II, 450.

## Chapter 6

### Lightness Depresseth Us

1. See Bernard H. Newdigate, *Michael Drayton and His Crude* (Oxford, 1941), p. 56.
2. W. A. Murray, "Donne and Paracelsus: An Essay in Interpretation." *RES*, XXV (1949), 115-123; p. 120.
3. *Ibid.*, p. 119.
4. See Empson, *Ambiguity*, pp. 51 and 140.
5. See Hayward's valuable note, *op. cit.*, p. 767.
6. See Th. H. Van de Velde, *Ideal Marriage*: *Its Physiology and Technique,* trans. Stella Browne (New York, 1930), p. 248; and Norman Hare, ed., *Encyclopaedia of Sexual Knowledge* (New York, 1937), p. 200.
7. See Kökeritz, *loc. cit.*, p. 161.
8. See *horn* and *short* in Partridge, *op. cit.*
9. See E. M. W. Tillyard and C. S. Lewis, *The Personal Heresy*: *A Controversy* (London, 1939).
10. C. S. Lewis, "Donne and Love Poetry in the Seventeenth Century," in *Seventeenth Century Studies Presented to Sir Herbert Grierson* (Oxford, 1938), 64-84; p. 74.
11. See Joan Bennett, "The Love Poetry of John Donne: A Reply to Mr. C. S. Lewis," *Seventeenth Century Studies,* pp. 85-104.
12. See George R. Potter, ed., *A Sermon Preached at Lincoln's Inn by John Donne* (Stanford, 1946), p. 65.
13. *Ibid.*, pp. 30 f.
14. See Hayward, *op. cit.*, p. 751.
15. Alford, IV, 318.
16. *Ibid.*, IV, 179.
17. *Ibid.*, IV, 70.
18. *Ibid.*, I, 335.
19. *Ibid.*, IV, 28.
20. *Ibid.*, I, 352.
21. *Idem;* cf. Bernard Alves Pereira, *La Doctrine du Mariage Selon Saint Augustin* (Paris, 1930), pp. 26-32.

22. Alford, IV, 22 f.
23. See Alves Pereira, *op. cit.,* pp. 66-69.
24. Alford, IV, 28.
25. See Alves Pereira, *op. cit.,* pp. 95-98.
26. See Benham, *loc. cit.,* pp. 273-281.
27. Hayward, *op. cit.,* p. 691
28. *Ibid.,* p. 734.
29. See Smith, *op. cit.,* p. 6.
30. "The Crosse," l. 58.
31. "The Litanie," ll. 188f.
32. "A Hymne to Christ, at the Authors last going into Germany," l. 28.
33. Alford, I, 448.
34. Hayward, *op. cit.,* p. 584.
35. See Deborah Bacon, *The Dream and the Poem: A Study of Freudian Symbolism in the Imagery of John Donne* (unpublished Columbia Master's essay, 1948).
36. See William Empson, "Donne and the Rhetorical Tradition," *Kenyon Review,* XI (1949), 571-587; pp. 579-587. Cf. his anticipation of this approach, in *Pastoral,* pp. 75-77.
37. "The good-morrow," ll. 12-14.
38. "The Canonization," ll. 5-9.
39. "Breake of Day," ll. 17f.
40. Valentine epithalamium, ll. 23 f.
41. Johnson, *op. cit.,* p. 22.
42. Brooks, *Urn,* p. 17.
43. Alford, V, 111.
44. "Holy Sonnet V," ll. 1f.
45. Alford, I, 502.
46. *Ibid.,* IV, 577.

# Bibliography

Alford, Henry, ed., *The Works of John Donne . . .*, 6 vol. (London, 1839).

Allen, Don Cameron, "Donne's Phoenix," *MLN*, LXII (1947), 340-342.

——————, "John Donne's Knowledge of Renaissance Medicine," *JEGP*, XLII (1943), 322-342.

Alves Pereira, Bernard, *La Doctrine du Mariage Selon Saint Augustin* (Paris, 1930).

Bacon, Deborah, *The Dream and the Poem: A Study of Freudian Symbolism in the Imagery of John Donne* (unpublished Columbia Master's essay, 1948).

Benham, Allen R., "The Myth of John Donne the Rake," pp. 273-281 in *Renaissance Studies in Honor of Hardin Craig*, ed. Baldwin Maxwell, *et al.* (Stanford, 1941).

Bennett, Joan, "The Love Poetry of John Donne: A Reply to Mr. C. S. Lewis," pp. 85-104 in *Seventeenth Century Studies Presented to Sir Herbert Grierson* (Oxford, 1938).

Bethell, S. L., "Two Streams from Helicon," Part III, *The New English Weekly*, XXVIII (1945-46), 213 f.

Brooks, Cleanth, *Modern Poetry and the Tradition* (Chapel Hill, 1939).

——————, *The Well Wrought Urn: Studies in the Structure of Poetry* (New York, 1947).

Coffin, Charles M., *John Donne and the New Philosophy* (New York, 1937).

Doggett, Frank A., "Donne's Platonism," *Sewanee Review*, XLII (1934), 272-92.

Donne, John, *Biathanatos* (facsimile text of undated first issue of first edition; New York, 1930). For other Donne texts, see Alford, Garrod, Grierson, Hayward, Merrill, Potter, and Smith.

Dryden, John, *The Critical and Miscellaneous Prose Works . . .*, ed. Edmond Malone, 3 vol. (London, 1800).

Duncan, Edgar H., "Donne's Alchemical Figures," *ELH*, IX (1942), 257-285.

Eliot, T. S., "John Donne," *The Nation & the Athenaeum*, XXXIII

(1923), 331 f.

――――――, *Selected Essays*: 1917-1932 (New York, 1932).

Emerson, Ralph Waldo, *Poems* (London, 1914).

Empson, William "Donne and the Rhetorical Tradition," *Kenyon Review*, XI (1949), 571-587.

――――――, *Seven Types of Ambiguity*, Second Edition (New York, 1947).

――――――, *Some Version of Pastoral* (London, 1935).

Fausset, Hugh I'Anson, *John Donne*: *A Study in Discord* (London, 1924).

Finney, Gretchen L., "Ecstasy and Music in Seventeenth-Century England," *JHI*, VIII (1947), 153-186.

Freeman, Rosemary, *English Emblem Books* (London, 1948).

Freud, Sigmund, *A General Introduction to Psycho-Analysis*, trans. Joan Riviere (New York, 1935).

Garrod, H. W. ed., *John Donne*: *Poetry* & *Prose* (Oxford, 1946).

Grierson, Herbert J. C., *The Poems of John Donne*, 2 vol. (Oxford, 1912).

Haire, Norman, ed., *Encyclopaedia of Sexual Knowledge* (New York, 1937).

Hayward, John, ed., *John Donne . . .: Complete Poetry and Selected Prose* (London, 1930).

Herford, C. H., and Percy and Evelyn Simpson, ed., *Ben Jonson*, 8 vol. (Oxford, 1925-47).

Herrick, Robert, *Works . . .*, ed. A. W. Pollard, 2 vol., Revised Edition (London, 1898).

Hughes, Merritt Y., "Kidnapping Donne," pp. 61-89 in *Essays in Criticism, Second Series* (*University of California Publications in English*, IV; Berkeley, 1934).

――――――, "The Lineage of 'The Extasie,' " *MLR*, XXVII (1932), 1-5.

Johnson, Samuel, *The Works . . .*, ed. Arthur Murphy, 12 vol. (London, 1801).

Jonas, Leah, *The Divine Science*: *The Aesthetic of Some Representative Seventeenth Century English Poets* (New York, 1940).

Jonson, Ben, *Ben Jonson's Conversations with William Drummond of Hawthornden*, ed. R. F. Patterson (London, 1923).

Jordan, Richard, *Handbuch der Mittelenglischen Grammatik*, Part 1, Second Edition (Heidelberg, 1934).

# Bibliography

Kökeritz, Helge, "Shakespeare's Pronunciation," *Moderna Språk,* XLIII (1949), 149-168.

Lederer, Josef, "John Donne and the Emblematic Practice," *RES,* XXII (1946), 182-200.

Legouis, Pierre, *Donne the Craftsman: An Essay Upon the Structure of the Songs and Sonnets* (Paris, 1928).

Leishman, J. B., *The Metaphysical Poets: Donne, Herbert, Vaughan, Traherne* (Oxford, 1934).

Lewis, C. S., "Donne and Love Poetry in the Seventeenth Century," pp. 64-84 in *Seventeenth Century Studies Presented to Sir Herbert Grierson* (Oxford, 1938).

――――――, and E. M. W. Tillyard, *The Personal Heresy*. See Tillyard.

Merrill, Charles E., ed., Donne's *Letters to Severall Persons of Honour* (New York, 1910).

Murray, W. A., "Donne and Paracelsus: An Essay in Interpretation," *RES,* XXV (1949), 115-123.

Newdigate, Bernard H., *Michael Drayton and His Circle* (Oxford, 1941).

Partridge, Eric, *Shakespeare's Bawdy: A Literary & Psychological Essay and a Comprehensive Glossary* (New York, 1948).

Paull, H. M., *Literary Ethics: A Study in the Growth of the Literary Conscience* (New York, 1929).

Potter, George R., ed., *A Sermon Preached at Lincoln's Inn by John Donne* (Stanford, 1946).

――――――, "Donne's *Extasie,* Contra Legouis," *PQ,* XV (1936), 247-253.

Ransom, John Crowe, "Honey and Gall," *Southern Review,* VI (1940), 2-19.

――――――, *The New Criticism* (Norfolk, Conn.; 1941).

Richards, I. A., *The Philosophy of Rhetoric* (New York, 1936).

Rugoff, Milton A., *Donne's Imagery: A Study in Creative Sources* (New York, 1939).

Shakespeare, William, *The Complete Works . . .,* ed. George Lyman Kittredge (Boston, 1936).

Simpson, Evelyn M., *A Study of the Prose Works of John Donne,* Second Edition (Oxford, 1948).

Simpson, Percy and Evelyn, and C. H. Herford, ed., *Ben Jonson.* See Herford.

Smith, Logan Pearsall, *Donne's Sermons: Selected Passage with an Essay* (Oxford, 1919).

Spurgeon, Caroline, *Shakespeare's Imagery and What It Tells Us* (Cambridge, 1935).

Stauffer, Donald A., *The Nature of Poetry* (New York, 1946).

Sterne, Laurence, *Tristram Shandy,* ed. James A. Work (New York, 1940).

Tate, Allen, *Reason in Madness: Critical Essays* (New York, 1941).

Thompson, Francis, *Shelley* (New York, 1909).

Thurber, James, *Let Your Mind Alone! and Other More or Less Inspirational Pieces* (New York, 1937).

Tillyard, E. M. W., and C. S. Lewis, *The Personal Heresy: A Controversy* (London, 1939).

Tuve, Rosemond, *Elizabethan and Metaphysical Imagery: Renaissance Poetic and Twentieth-Century Critics* (Chicago, 1947).

Van de Velde, Th. H., *Ideal Marriage: Its Physiology and Technique,* trans. Stella Browne (New York, 1930).

Warren, Austin. See Wellek.

Wellek, René, "The Concept of Baroque in Literary Scholarship," *Journal of Aesthetics and Art Crticism,* V (1946), 77-109.

——————, and Austin Warren, *Theory of Literature* (New York, 1949).

Williamson, George, review of Rugoff, *MLN,* LVI (1941), 626-628.

——————, "Textual Difficulties in the Interpretation of Donne's Poetry," *MP,* XXXVIII (1940), 37-72.

Wyld, H. C., *A History of Modern Colloquial English,* Third Edition (Oxford, 1936).

Yeats, W. B., *Essays,* Revised Edition (New York, 1924).

# *Appendix*

## EMPSON'S IDLE TEARS

REGARDING THE WEEPING valediction, I quote from Empson: "Those critics who say the poem is sincere, . . . and therefore must have been written to poor Anne, know not what they do" (*Ambiguity*, p. 139). I would agree with this statement as it stands here, but not with the meaning which Empson's context gives it. He is not, as might appear to be the case, attacking the sinceritas heresy; indeed, Empson is more biographical in this analysis than I should care to be. There are formidable ambiguities in Empson's own style, but I gather that his contention might be stated like this: Donne in his own person is addressing a woman he loves; "the language of the poem is shot through with a suspicion . . . that when he is gone she will be unfaithful to him" (p. 139); consequently, the woman addressed would not (or, at least, should not) have been his wife.

I have no interest in whitewashing Donne's (or Anne's) personal life, and I certainly cannot deny, if I would, that cynicism may occur in Donne, or that tenderness and cynicism may appear side by side in the same poem. All I am contending is that the mixture does not occur in this particular poem of Donne's, and that the poem is consequently Petrarchan in tone (to the extent that *Petrarchan* means anything).

Empson adduces a number of faintly possible ambiguities which add up to an ironic ambiguity of attitude: the lady's impending fall represents a forthcoming lapse in fidelity, rather than (as I would have it) a descent into meaningless existence. If Empson is sympathizing with the poet, his fears are unfounded. Such an interpretation imports into this poem an idea which belongs (and functionally) to the Mourning valediction: that pedestrian love-affairs dissipate into nothingness under the test of absence. Here, to be sure, the lovers become nothing, and absence is the cause, but we are hardly justified in carrying the figure to its logical conclusions. Let me demonstrate the dangers of such a procedure, by once more citing a figure from the Mourning valediction. In that poem the lovers' united souls, despite their enforced physical separation, undergo merely an expansion, not a breach; the process is likened to that of beating gold into infinitesimally thin foil. Suppose we carried the idea to its logical conclusions; we'd get something like this: an expansion of the type described must result in such tenuousness that it might as well be a breach. Obviously, such a thought is inappropriate to the poem (as considered carefully), but it is highly applicable in another context: in a passage in *Biathanatos* Donne likens the willfull misinterpretation of the Scriptures to the process of beating gold into foil. The result is that the "tincture and colour of gold" is retained, but "all the waight and estimation" is lost (p. 155 of the undated first issue of the first edition).

# *Index*

(A title and first-line index of Donne's poems analyzed or commented on in entirety or in part.)

## I. TITLES

## II.  FIRST LINES

Like one who'in her third widdowhood doth professe [To Mr. Rowland Woodward]

Looke to me faith, and look to my faith, God; [Elegie upon the untimely death of the incomparable Prince Henry]

Man is the World, and death th' Ocean, [Elegie on the Lady Marckham]

Marke but this flea, and marke in this, [The Flea]

My name engrav'd herein, [A Valediction: of my name, in the window]

Nothing could make me sooner to confesse [Of the Progresse of the Soule]

Now thou hast lov'd me one whole day, [Womans constancy]

O thou which to search out the secret parts [To Mr. S. B.]

Oh doe not die, for I shall hate [A Feaver]

Our storme is past, and that storms tyrannous rage, [The Calme]

*Salute the last and everlasting day*, [Ascension]

Show me deare Christ, thy spouse, so bright and clear. [Holy Sonnet XVIII]

Since I am coming to that Holy roome, [Hymne to God my God, in my sicknesse]

Since she whom I lov'd hath payd her last debt [Holy Sonnet XVII]

Sir; though (I thank God for it) I do hate [Satyre II]

Some that have deeper digg'd loves Myne then I, [Loves Alchymie]

Sweetst love, I do not goe, [Song]

The Sun-beames in the East are spred, [Epithalamion made at Lincolnes Inne

This twilight of two years, not past nor next, [To the Countesse of Bedford]

Thou art repriv'd old year, thou shalt not die, [Epithalamion]

Tis the yeares midnight, and it is the dayes, [A nocturnall upon S. Lucies day, being the shortest day]

'Tis true, 'tis day; what though it be? [Breake of day]

T'have written then, when you writ, seem'd to mee [To the Countesse of Bedford]

Twice or thrice had I loved thee [Aire and Angels]

Upon this Primrose hill, [The Primrose]

# ERRATA

P. 156: for ['l ɔɪ ə n z]
read [ləɪ' ənz]

for [l ɔɪ n z]
read [ləɪnz]